PRIESTHOOD

THE LOVE OF THE HEART OF JESUS

EDITED BY
JOHN PATRICK STOKELY

Priesthood Anthology
Saint Charles Borromeo Seminary
100 East Wynnewood Road
Wynnewood, PA 19096

ISBN: 978-0-578-07961-5

Cover design by John Patrick Stokely
Photo credit: Rev. Daniel Good

PRINTED IN THE UNITED STATES OF AMERICA

CONTENTS

ACKNOWLEDGEMENTS

Thank you so very much to:

Monsignor Michael Magee, the faculty moderator of this project, who guided me and taught me so much throughout these past two years.

Monsignor Joseph Prior, the former Rector of Saint Charles Borromeo Seminary, who continually encouraged me and assisted greatly in the early phases of this project.

Father Shaun Mahoney, the current Rector of Saint Charles Borromeo Seminary, who has supported me tremendously in this endeavor, both in vision and resources.

Nicholas Barnes, Scott Belina, Brian Fallon, Phillip Halladay, Victor Ingalls, Alex Roche, and Dan Shaughnessy, my brother seminarians and friends, who assisted greatly in the planning and coordination of this project.

My parents, Patrick and Joan, and my family who have always supported, encouraged, and prayed for me.

INTRODUCTION

It is my great joy and privilege to present to you this anthology about the Priesthood of Jesus Christ.

I owe immense gratitude to Jesus Christ, the High Priest, for his abundant blessings upon me and this project, which has come to completion after more than two years.

In October 2008, with the help of Monsignor Michael Magee and seven seminarians from Saint Charles Borromeo Seminary, the Pontifical North American College, and Kenrick-Glennon Seminary, the formal process of creating this book began. Since then, through the generosity and support of so many Priests and Bishops, this anthology has become a reality.

May you experience the love of the heart of Jesus through these reflections, which I hope will bring us all to a deeper appreciation and love for Jesus Christ, the Church, and His Priesthood.

John Patrick Stokely
November 4, 2010
Feast of Saint Charles Borromeo

FRANCIS CARDINAL ARINZE

Cardinal Francis Arinze, Prefect emeritus of the Congregation of Divine Worship and the Discipline of the Sacraments, was born on November 1, 1932 in Eziowelle, a city of the Archdiocese of Onitsha, Nigeria. At the age of fifteen, he began his secondary studies at the All Hallowa (All Saints) Seminary of Nuewi, studies which he concluded in 1950 at Enugu. For the following two years he taught at the same seminary until 1953, when he took up philosophy studies at Bigard Memorial Seminary at Enugu. In 1955 he began to take courses in theology at the Pontifical Urban University. Only three years later he was ordained to the Priesthood during a ceremony which took place at the church of the Pontifical Urban University in Rome on November 23, 1958.

From 1961-1962, he was professor of liturgy and also taught logic and basic philosophy at Bigard Memorial Seminary at Enugu. He was then appointed regional secretary for Catholic education for the eastern part of his country. When transferred to London, he took courses at the Institute of Pedagogy, earning a diploma in 1964.

On July 6, 1965 he was appointed to the titular church of Fissiana and named coadjutor to the Archbishop of Onitsha. On August 29, 1965 he was consecrated Bishop. Only two years after he was asked to take over the pastoral government of the archdiocese, and on June 26, 1967 he was named Archbishop.

In 1979 his brother Bishops elected him president of the Catholic Bishops' Conference of Nigeria, which post he filled until 1984, when John Paul II asked him to head as pro-president the Secretariat for Non-Christians (now the Pontifical Council for Interreligious Dialogue).

He remained Archbishop of Onitsha until April 1985, while awaiting the nomination of his successor to assume the pastoral administration of the Archdiocese. In addition, in 1982 he was elected vice-president for Africa of the United Bible Society.

On October 1, 2002 he was nominated Prefect of the Congregation of Divine Worship and the Discipline of the Sacraments. Cardinal Arinze became Prefect emeritus of the Congregation of Divine Worship and the Discipline of the Sacraments on December 9, 2008.

The Priesthood:
A Gift of the Sacred Heart of Jesus

Jesus Christ, the Second Person in the Blessed Trinity, for love of us and for our salvation, came down from heaven. By his entire earthly life, and especially by the paschal mysteries of his death, burial, resurrection and ascension, he did the work of our salvation. Our Eternal High Priest, he is both Priest and victim.

The immense love of the Sacred Heart of Jesus for his Church and for all humanity helps to explain the great gift he made of the Priesthood to his Church and to the world. That a man is given a share in the Priesthood of Christ so that he can celebrate, preach, and gather the people of God together, is a reason for wonder, thanksgiving and joy. A word on each of these three offices of the Priest will be useful.

The Priest is ordained to celebrate the saving mysteries of Christ. He is at the height of his calling when at the altar he celebrates the Eucharistic Sacrifice, the sacramental representation of the Sacrifice of Calvary. He does this *in persona Christi*. His way of celebrating should be such that the faith of believers is nourished and they are sent home on fire to live and share the faith. He also baptizes, forgives sins in the name of Christ, anoints the sick and blesses the marriages of the followers of Jesus. The Priest imposes his anointed hands on people and invokes on them the blessings of the Father, the Son and the Holy Spirit. He offers people's prayers to God and brings down God's blessings on them.

The ministry of the Word is also entrusted to the Priest. He proclaims the Word of God to the people, especially in the liturgical assembly. He explains it to the people in the homily and relates the proclaimed word to the realities of life on earth today. His homily is not a parade of hypotheses. It is not a show of learning. It is not theological acrobatics. It is an authoritative exposition of our Catholic faith which nourishes and builds up the people of God. Because the Priest is on fire with the Gospel of salvation in Jesus Christ, he can inspire. Our Catholic faith is not a doubtful or controverted matter. It is not a question of yes, no, may be, sometimes, perhaps, or let us find out the majority view or the public opinion as expressed by the daily influential newspapers and magazines. No. Our faith is built upon Jesus Christ. He is the same yesterday, today, and forever (cf Heb 13:8). We know in whom we have believed (cf 2 Tim 1:12).

The Priest is also sent to gather the people of God together under the authority and directions of his diocesan Bishop. The Catholic community is a visible spiritual flock which needs for its leadership a man who is the representative of Christ, Head and Shepherd. The authority of the Priest in the Church comes from Christ. The Priest does not draw attention to himself. He does not project himself. He is a mirror through which people should see Christ. When a mirror draws attention to itself, then it is dirty and it is time to clean it. The Priest is Christ's ambassador, and that says much already. And he works in unity and harmony with the Bishop and his brother Priests.

There is no other religious family in history that has a minister quite like the Priest in the Catholic Church. We owe the Sacred Heart of Jesus immense gratitude for his great gift of the Priesthood.

+Francis Cardinal Arinze
Vatican City
27 May, 2010

Rev. Dennis J. Billy, C.Ss.R.

Dennis J. Billy, C.Ss.R. is a Redemptorist Priest of the Baltimore Province. He was professed in 1977 and ordained in 1980. For more than twenty years he was Professor of the history of moral theology and Christian spirituality at the Alphonsian Academy of The Pontifical Lateran University in Rome. He is currently professor, scholar-in-residence, and holder of the John Cardinal Krol Chair of Moral Theology at Saint Charles Borromeo Seminary. He also serves as the Karl Rahner Professor of Catholic Theology at the Graduate Theological Foundation in Mishawaka, Indiana. Father Billy holds a Th.D. in Church History from Harvard Divinity School, an S.T.D. in Spirituality from The Pontifical University of Saint Thomas, and a D.Min. in Spiritual Direction from the Graduate Theological Foundation. He has also pursued higher studies at the University of Toronto and The Catholic University of Louvain. He has authored or edited more than 25 books and has published numerous articles in a variety of scholarly and popular journals. His most recent books include: C. S. Lewis on the Fullness of Life: Longing for Deep Heaven (Paulist Press, 2009) and The Beauty of the Eucharist: Voices from the Church Fathers (New City Press, 2010). Father Billy is also very active as a retreat director and a noted spiritual director.

Discerning a Call: Before the Seminary

During this year for Priests in honor of the 150th anniversary of the death of Saint Jean Vianney, I will personally be marking the 30th year of my Priestly ordination. I look back over the years with gratitude for my vocation and also a sense of wonder at how the Lord has worked in my life. Don't get me wrong. I have had my share of ups and downs in my life as a Priest. What Priest doesn't? At the same time, I am humbled by the way God has led me in my vocation and ministry and used to lead others to Him.

As I look back over the years, my thoughts turn to the time before I entered the seminary, to a time when I was first discerning God's call. Behind every vocation to the Priesthood lies a story about a man's relationship with the Lord. Each story is unique, yet also strangely familiar; it is deeply personal, yet also universal. It would be impossible for me to relate all the factors that went into my decision to enter the seminary and begin the long journey to ordination. What I would like to do in these pages is simply reflect upon some of the occurrences in my life that led me to take the first step in saying, "I think God may be calling me to become a Priest." My reason for doing so is to convey a sense that if God could call *me* to the Priesthood, He could call almost anyone. I didn't go looking for my vocation. It found me – and it was all the Lord's doing.

When I was a young boy growing up in the late 50s and early 60s in Saint Christopher's parish in Staten Island, the forgotten borough of New York, thoughts of the Priesthood were far from my mind. Back then, Staten Island was a very Catholic environment (and largely still is). My family practiced the faith, but was not overly religious. We went to Mass on Sundays. My brothers and sister and I were sent to the local Catholic school, where we were educated by Presentation Sisters. I entered Saint Christopher's School in 1959 before Vatican II and left it in 1967, a couple of years after it ended. I remember going to the 9 A. M. children's Mass every Sunday morning being led by nuns dressed in full habit with the boys seated on the right side of the aisle and the girls on the left. I also remember having to bring in a note signed by my parents whenever I was absent. The Mass, of course, was in Latin. When the opportunity arose at the age of 10, I became an altar boy, along with 95% of the other boys in my class.

I remember going to altar boy practice during the summer before I entered the 5th grade and being anxious about whether I would be able to say the Latin responses at the appropriate times. For a young boy back then, being an altar boy was something of a badge of honor. It involved a lot of work, like getting up extra early on a weekday to walk the half mile to Church and serve the 7 A. M. Mass before school or staying after school to practice for the Holy Week services. But there were also a number of perks, like getting out of class every now and then to serve a funeral and our yearly summer outing to the amusement part in Lake Hopatcong, New Jersey.

Thoughts of the Priesthood must have entered my mind at some point during my grammar school years, but I can't say that it captured my imagination. The only time I remember giving it some thought was when a bunch of my friends and I got into serious trouble one day during recess. Sr. Mary Raphael, our fifth grade teacher, took us aside and scolded us, saying that she was disappointed in us, especially since one of us might one day become a Priest. She then proceeded to point at each one of us and to look us in the eyes. I was the last one upon whom her eyes fell. She then made us kneel down around her and ask God for forgiveness for what we had done. I can't remember what horrible thing we had done to deserve this scolding, but I distinctly remember wondering to myself afterwards if I was meant to be a Priest.

Such thoughts, however, did not stay with me for long. I had my sights on other things like building forts, forming secret clubs, exploring places outside the neighborhood, making up games, and playing sports (baseball was my favorite). That is not to say that the Lord wasn't giving me a reminder every now and then. My best friend entered the minor seminary after grammar school. In the years leading up to graduation, he would invite me from time to time to go with him to a vocation club meeting. I went with him a couple of times, but never thought of entering the seminary. I needed to grow up a bit before I could consider it a distinct possibility.

One memory that stays with me to this day has to do with the place where I lived on Jefferson Avenue. This street marked the border between my parish and the neighboring parish on Dongan Hills, Saint Ann's. I always used to joke that I could go to the neighboring parish by simply crossing the street. Whenever I looked up Jefferson Avenue, I could see in the distance at the top of Todt Hill a large white mansion that happened to be a seminary for the Sacalabrini Fathers. This house had a large, looming presence in my mind throughout my childhood. Although I never seriously thought of entering the seminary, my friends and I would often hike up there to explore the surrounding woods, climb in its tall trees, or play on its ball field. The seminary, in my boyhood mind, was a place for adventure and play rather than a place for prayer and study.

After grammar school, I entered to the local Catholic high school. My four years at Monsignor Farrell High School in Oakwood were dedicated pretty much to two things: study and running (and not necessarily in that order). I ran Cross Country, Indoor, and Outdoor Track for all four years and was elected Captain in my senior year. I was taught by Diocesan Priests, Irish Christian Brothers, and a small group of dedicated laity. I received a top notch education at Farrell and was eventually able to get into some of the top schools in the country. I also remember thinking at the time that Cross Country and Track had taught me the importance of self-discipline and perseverance in life. Long-distance running had served me well in more ways than one.

As far as my faith was concerned, I would have to say that I really didn't pay all that much attention to it. Being a Catholic from birth, I just took it for granted. I didn't question my faith very much, but simply went along with the flow. I still went to Sunday Mass and made sure I made it to Church on holy days. However, I can't say that I had any real personal investment in it. Nor did I understand it, especially with all the changes taking place in the years immediately following the Council. The Catholic faith didn't excite or grab hold of me the way other things did. I was just a typical teenager who was focused on doing well in school and in sports.

At the same time, I would have to say that the quiet witness of the Priests and brothers who taught me had affected me deeply. I wasn't necessarily conscious of it at the time, but I can honestly say that moving from a Catholic grammar school to a Catholic high school, from the strict discipline of the sisters to the close supervision of the Priests and brothers was an important step for me on the way to manhood. *Vir fidelis*, "The Faithful Man," was my high school's motto. Although I can't say that my faith meant a whole lot to me during my time there, I must admit that the Priests and brothers were molding my soul in their own quiet ways and preparing me for some of the rough times ahead. *The Cornerstone* was the name of my high school yearbook. I look back on those years as the time when the cornerstone of my faith was quietly laid in small, seemingly insignificant ways.

In much of the world and the United States, those years (1967-71) were a time of protest and rebellion against the establishment. It was the Vietnam era, the excitement of Woodstock, and the dawning of "the Age of Aquarius." Jesus was being depicted as an anti-establishment rock star who had more in common with the Beatles than the Brothers of the Christian Schools. Amidst all of the craziness, I could easily have found myself falling in with a crowd that tried more to rock the establishment than look for the good in it. The Priests and brothers at Farrell gave me and my fellow classmates a safe environment in which we could learn, grow, and strive to realize our dreams.

After high school graduation in 1971, I worked the summer as a messenger boy for a Wall Street investment firm in Manhattan called Dryfoos and Company. On August 25th, the day before my 18th birthday, I was sent to deliver a package to the New Amsterdam Press on 125th Street and 8th Avenue in Harlem. After dropping off the package, I was making my way back to the 7th Avenue line on 125th Street and was held up at knifepoint by four men. At that moment, my whole life literally flashed before my eyes. One got hold of me from behind; another put a knife to my throat; another took my wallet out of my back pocket; and another took my watch off my wrist. I thought I was going to be killed in broad daylight, before a crowd of passive onlookers, and all for a cheap watch and the few dollars I had in my wallet. The four men, who were probably in their early twenties, took my belongings and taunted me, before they ran down the street and disappeared into the crowd. Lucky for me, they had forgotten to check my pockets, for I had enough change to buy a subway token and make my way back to the office. Once there, my boss calmed me down, gave me some water, and sent me home for the day. I can't recall if we reported the crime to the police.

That night I woke up shaking and in a cold sweat in the middle of the night. What a way to celebrate my 18th birthday – – with a bout of post-traumatic shock! The experience left me deeply wounded in mind and spirit. For the first time in my life I had had first hand experience of the fragility of life. I felt violated and insecure. Death was no longer something that happened to someone else, but something close-up and personal. It was something that could really happen – to me! The experience of a stranger putting a knife to my neck changed me forever. I knew I would never be the same. I brought that experience with me when I began college a few weeks later. I began to see my life in a different light. I realized that I could no longer take anything for granted: not my life, my family, my friends, not even my faith. I started to probe and questions things in a way I had never done before.

A few weeks later, I matriculated as a freshman at Dartmouth College in Hanover, New Hampshire. I feel a little embarrassed now having to admit that during my first year there I seriously considered leaving the Catholic Church. This was the first time in my life that I was away from my family and friends for any extended period of time. Coming out of a Catholic elementary and high school system, it was also the first time in my life that I found some of my most basic assumptions about life, about religion, about God challenged and put to the test – not so much by my professors (although one or two of them managed to get under my skin), but from my classmates. Being in an environment, where not everyone was Catholic, where not every one was Christian, where not every one believed in God, and where some people did not seem to believe in anything was very confusing to me and, easily influenced by my peers, I must admit, I felt a little overwhelmed by it all.

At first, I played the role of an apologist and tried to defend what I had always been told to believe. That didn't last very long. The arguments of my classmates were too good for me. I could not keep up with them and, after a while, they even started to make sense to me. I had no answer that would satisfy them. My answers did not even satisfy me. Then some of my Catholic classmates, from whom I expected more than mere token support, themselves began to change. Some started smoking marijuana. Others experimented with some of the Eastern religions; others, with Christian fundamentalism. Others stopped calling themselves Catholic, more, I suppose, out of lack of interest than anything else. Others stopped believing in God altogether. My close brush with death the summer before didn't help matters. I wondered why God would allow such an awful thing to happen. I wondered why there was so much evil in the world and wondered why God didn't seem to care. To be honest, I felt myself drifting in the general same direction with everyone else – *away* from the Catholic Church.

And I probably would have were it not for Father Bill Nolan, who at the time was the chaplain at Aquinas House, the Catholic Center at Dartmouth. During the second trimester of my freshman year, I found myself wandering into Father Bill's office about once every week or so, mainly to lock horns with him (I can be pretty engaging when I want to). I gave him all my newfound arguments against God and religion, together with all the things that I could think of that were wrong with the Catholic Church (my list, by this time, had become pretty long), and I tried to convince him that my decision to leave the Catholic Church was mature and well thought out, that I was following my conscience and doing the right thing. I was really looking for a fight. I figured that if I argued with him long enough he would eventually do either one of two things: give up or explode. Either way I would have won. And, if he exploded, well that would have been just one more reason for me to leave the Church.

The trouble was I could not get Father Bill to argue back. He explained the Church's teaching as best he could. But, other than that, all he did was keep on saying week after week, time and time again in his deep voice that exuded confidence, "Now, Dennis, be sure you know what you're rejecting before you toss it all away." After our second or third meeting, I was beginning to get a little annoyed with his unwillingness to engage my arguments head on. I could not draw him into the fray of battle. He just sat there and smiled at me. How do you fight with someone who refuses to fight back? Turning one's cheek in what was supposed to be a serious argument was going a bit too far. "The Golden Rule," so I thought, did not apply in matters of such consequence. To tell you the truth, Father Bill took me by surprise with his calm and gentle manner. And, deep down inside, I knew he was right. I could not reject my Catholic faith – at least not then – because, after my Catholic upbringing and education, I really did not know what it was all about (and I certainly did not understand it). For all my life, I had simply taken it for granted. And since I could no longer do that, I decided to do something about it.

Over the space of the next six weeks, I read the documents of the Second Vatican Council slowly and with great interest from cover to cover. I still have the copy of the Abbot edition that I read, and I go back to it often to examine all the notes I made in the margins and all the things I underlined because they impressed me so much. I remember, for example, being particularly taken up by the idea of Christ's Body being a complex reality with different degrees of incorporation. I was also very much impressed with the image of the Church as "The People of God," with the expressed willingness of the Church to enter into dialogue with other Christian and non-Christian faiths, and with its repeated emphasis on the dignity of the human person.

I was deeply affected by what I read. It is difficult to explain in words, but after reading the documents of the Second Vatican Council, I felt as if I was experiencing my faith with different eyes, as if for the first time. The pieces were beginning to fit together. It all started to make sense to me. I was beginning to feel something I had not felt in a long time, if ever: at home in my faith. I was no longer taking it for granted. I was beginning to take responsibility for what I believed. And, most importantly, I was beginning to experience God as a personal presence in my life. That is not to say that all my difficulties with the Catholic faith simply melted away. My arguments and objections were not all answered, not by a long shot. But I can honestly say that from pieces strewn throughout the various documents of the Council, I was able to come up with a vision of the Catholic faith that I could live with and readily accept. At the end of that six week period during my freshman year in college, I consciously chose to remain a member of the Catholic faith – and I have never regretted my decision, not for a single moment.

I look upon my freshman year in college as a quiet time of conversion. During that year I was thinking deep thoughts (about as deep as I could go at the time) and experiencing my Catholic faith, as if for the first time. Towards the end of the year, I had an official group interview with Father Bill (all throughout the year, he had been slowly making his way through the freshman class in small gatherings of five or six). Toward the end of this meeting, we were each handed an index card and told to write down our name, our college address, our major (if we had one yet), and what we wanted to be. I surprised myself (and probably Father Bill as well – although, perhaps not) when I put down that I wanted to be a Priest. I was ordained some eight years later.

BISHOP MICHAEL F. BURBIDGE

Michael F. Burbidge was born June 16, 1957, in Philadelphia, Pennsylvania, the second son of Francis and Shirley (Lilley) Burbidge and brother of Francis Burbidge, Jr. He attended Catholic grade schools and graduated from Cardinal O'Hara High School, Springfield, Pennsylvania in 1975. From high school he went to Saint Charles Borromeo Seminary and was ordained a Priest of the Archdiocese of Philadelphia by John Cardinal Krol in 1984.

Bishop Burbidge holds a B.A. in Philosophy and a M.A. in Theology from Saint Charles Borromeo Seminary, a M.A. in Education Administration from Villanova University and a doctorate in Education Administration from Immaculata College.

Father Michael Burbidge's first Priestly assignment was as Parochial Vicar of Saint Bernard Church in Philadelphia, where he served for two years. From 1986-1992, he was on the faculties, successively, of Cardinal O'Hara High School, Archbishop Wood High School and Saint Charles Borromeo Seminary, where he also served as Dean of Students.

In 1992, Father Burbidge was named Administrative Secretary to His Eminence Anthony Cardinal Bevilacqua, Archbishop of Philadelphia, and served in that capacity until 1999. He was made

Honorary Prelate to His Holiness Pope John Paul II in 1998 with the title of Monsignor.

Monsignor Burbidge was appointed Rector of Saint Charles Borromeo Seminary in 1999. He served as Rector until 2004. In 2002, he was ordained an Auxiliary Bishop of Philadelphia.

On June 8, 2006, Pope Benedict XVI named Bishop Burbidge the fifth Bishop of the Diocese of Raleigh. He was installed in Raleigh on August 4.

Bishop Burbidge serves on the Committee on Priorities and Plans, the Administrative Committee as well as the Committee on Clergy, Consecrated Life and Vocations of the United States Conference of Catholic Bishops (USCCB). Additionally, he is a member of the USCCB's Committee on Migration. He also serves on the Conformity Review Team for the Catechism of the Catholic Church. In June 2009, Bishop Burbidge was elected to The Catholic University of America Board of Trustees and serves on its Seminary Committee. In addition, he is a member of the Board of Trustees of Saint Charles Borromeo Seminary and since 2006, has been a member of The Papal Foundation Board of Trustees and currently serves as its Secretary. Bishop Burbidge is also a member of the Episcopal Advisory Boards for the National Conference of Diocesan Vocation Directors, the Catholic Education Foundation and Catholic Athletes for Christ.

Walking Humbly with God as Priest and Servant

Choosing an Episcopal motto is one of the initial steps a new Bishop takes toward identifying his ministry. My motto is from Micah 6:8, in which we are reminded of the need to *"walk humbly with your God."* It is the virtue of humility which allows us to see ourselves as we are in the face of God. We recognize ourselves as creature not Creator. We understand our need for complete surrender and total dependence upon the One alone who can sustain us. Indeed, well before becoming a Bishop, I had been called to humility.

In first discerning the possibility that God was calling me to be a Priest, I was filled with great humility. I was well-aware of my many limitations and could easily identify with the prophet Jeremiah as I also felt too young and too weak *(Jeremiah 1: 5-9)*. With God's divine assistance, much prayer and spiritual guidance, I was able to understand that the Lord our God gives the strength and grace needed to all those He calls to follow Him. With profound trust in that reality one can only say, "Here I am, Lord, send me."

Our beloved Pope John Paul II eloquently spoke about God's call in his book, written on the occasion of his fiftieth anniversary as a Priest, *Gift and Mystery*. In the beginning of the book, Pope John Paul II states, "At its deepest level, every vocation to the Priesthood is a great mystery. It is a gift which infinitely transcends the individual." A vocation to the Priesthood is a mystery of divine election. As Jesus reminds us in the Gospel, "It was not you who chose me, but I who chose you and appointed you to go and bear fruit that will remain" *(John 15: 16-17)*. Priests find joy and serenity in knowing that it is God who calls, and our duty is simply to surrender to His holy will. Such a response requires humility, and this virtue needs to be reflected at every moment of our lives.

Throughout my Priesthood, I have been and remain ever thankful for the beautiful gift of being a Priest, as the one who stands in the very person of Jesus Christ as a living icon. I am in awe of the great privilege of bringing His presence to others in Word and Sacrament and in humble service. More than ever, the world is hungering and thirsting for that Presence!

I will always remember celebrating a parish Mass in which the seriously ill received the Sacrament of Anointing of the Sick. As I prepared to anoint one woman, it was very clear that she was suffering immensely. She must have sensed my sadness. She looked directly at me with a spiritual joy and said, "It's okay, Father. Just give me Jesus. Just give me Jesus."

With humility, it is essential that every Priest understand that people do not necessarily need us. They need the Lord. How blessed we are to be His instruments. Each day is a gift that allows us to give Jesus to our people. We must preach His Word and Truth with conviction, clarity and compassion. We must celebrate the Sacraments with reverence and joy. We must reach out to those who have grown lukewarm in the faith and assure them of God's infinite love and mercy. We must respond to the countless opportunities to serve the weak and needy in our midst, especially those who feel forgotten or unloved. Saint Paul teaches us how we must do this: with heartfelt compassion, kindness, humility, gentleness and peace, doing everything in the name of the Lord Jesus and giving thanks to the Father through Him and with the Holy Spirit *(Colossians 3: 12-15).*

In all these ways, we give Jesus to others. We will not always see the immediate results of our efforts. However, we can never grow discouraged. We rejoice in the Lord's promise, that He will use whatever we give Him in miraculous ways and, through us, will bear much fruit.

If we are to remain faithful to the call to give Jesus to others, it is essential that our intimate relationship with Him is our highest priority. Only when we draw ever closer to His Sacred Heart can we bring His love to others. Thus, our willingness to be with the Lord in fervent prayer is crucial in the life and ministry of every Priest. It is in those moments the Lord speaks to us and fills us with the gift of the Holy Spirit. In the Address opening the *Year for Priests* in June 2009, Our Holy Father Pope Benedict reminded Priests that our mission demands complete fidelity to Christ and constant union with Him. In other words, we must be holy Priests. Only then can we be the witnesses and servants He desires and His people need. Thus, as Saint Paul encourages us, we must understand our constant and great need "to confidently approach the Lord's throne to receive mercy and to find grace for timely help" *(Hebrews 4: 15-16).*

Throughout the Priesthood we find many occasions when we need "timely help." Sometimes, like Jesus, we will experience ridicule, opposition and outright rejection. We may be unfairly judged. Sometimes we are criticized or mocked for the beliefs we hold dear to our heart, beliefs that can never be compromised. It is only fitting that in the Ordination Rite, the Bishop places the bread and the chalice containing the wine mixed with water in the hands of the newly ordained and says, "Receive the oblation of the holy people, to be offered to God. Understand what you do, imitate what you celebrate, and conform your life to the mystery of the Lord's cross." Like Jesus, the Priest must give himself in service to the Lord and His people without counting the cost. The Priest must not run away from suffering and hardships on behalf of the Gospel. He must conform himself to the mystery of the cross in the sure and certain hope that we who die with Him will rise to newness of life and live with Him now and forever. In other words, the Priest must imitate the reality he celebrates every time he offers the Sacrifice of the Mass.

Upon my twenty-fifth anniversary as a Priest, I

reflected on the gift and mystery of Priesthood as lived out in my various assignments. I tried to determine the most important lesson I learned in each assignment. I wish to share those lessons with you and conclude by identifying the spiritual themes that unite them.

My first assignment as a newly-ordained Priest was in a large suburban parish. There were countless ministries and endless opportunities for pastoral service. A major lesson was taught to me by the parochial vicar with whom I lived, a Priest older and wiser. He told me that as a newly ordained Priest, the youth and young people will desire to spend time with you and you should respond. He stressed that I must never allow anything to interfere with the pastoral care of the sick. He emphasized the need to remember those parishioners who devoutly came to Church throughout their entire lives but could no longer do so because of illness. He stressed that they waited for their Priest each month to forgive their sins and bring them the Holy Eucharist. He concluded by saying, "Never, ever say you are too busy for this important Priestly obligation." Each Priest had over 50 visits a month. Never were the sick and homebound forgotten in the parish. It is a ministry that must remain dear to the heart of every Priest.

My next assignment in the Priesthood was teaching high school. Again, I learned a lesson about not forgetting those who need us the most. My mentor reminded me that teachers can have their egos boosted with the enthusiastic responses they receive from the intelligent, creative, athletic and popular students. Yet, teachers must be on the search for the student who sits alone in the cafeteria, the student who is not involved in any activities, the student struggling with grades and the student who seems simply out-of-place. The teacher, in imitation of Jesus the Perfect Teacher, must notice and reach out to the "outcast," the one others seem to forget so easily. The Priest must be the one who not only rejoices in those who come to him. The Priest must be the one who goes forth to embrace those in most need.

Two of my assignments returned me to the Seminary. There, I was privileged to serve men who shared the same call that the Lord had given to me. The Seminary is a place where spirituality is rightfully emphasized and the schedule of the day reflects a certain rhythm, beginning and ending with prayer. In parish life, the activities and pastoral services can sometimes be overwhelming and, unfortunately, lead to a neglect of the spiritual disciplines. My time at the Seminary as an administrator served to remind me of the great need to be disciplined in the basics of the spiritual life, over which nothing else can have priority. They include daily celebration of the Eucharist, fervent prayer including faithfulness to the Liturgy of the Hours, meditation upon God's holy Word, frequent Confession and devotion to Our Blessed Mother. Many times we can over-think or complicate our growth in the spiritual life. Yet, I believe strongly that the foundations and tools given to candidates in the Seminary must be preserved and treasured. They will always keep Priests on the right path.

A significant part of my Priestly ministry was spent in administration within the Archdiocesan Center, serving as Secretary to the Cardinal. Here, I learned vividly that the Church was much bigger than my parish, my diocese and my frame of reference. I began to have a clearer understanding of the Church as universal. My profession of faith took on a radically new meaning, especially as I said the words: one, *holy, catholic and apostolic.* How important it is for us to love and to pray for our Holy Father and Bishops and how important it is for us to understand that we are God's holy family, united with our brothers and sisters in Christ throughout our entire world. We must be extremely proud in being Catholic!

Throughout all of my assignments, there were some unifying themes. I humbly acknowledge that I often resisted most of my transfers at first. When I was ordained, I had hoped to be a parish Priest assigned to a large city parish. Miraculously, that happened just as I had planned. However, it was the only time in my Priesthood that things went according to my plan! When I was asked to teach high school, I begged not to be given this assignment. I never thought I could be a teacher. I ended up teaching high school and eventually I came to enjoy immensely this apostolate. When I was asked to return to the Seminary, I strongly requested the opportunity to stay in the education apostolate or return to parish life. I went back to the Seminary and now consider the assignments there to have been a tremendous privilege. I treasure those memories. My greatest fear came when I was asked to serve as the Cardinal's secretary. I stated my true belief that I lacked the competencies, training and skills for such an important role. I was fearful that I would never meet the expectations placed upon me. I was told to try it for two years. I held the position for seven years, and the Lord provided me with marvelous opportunities to see the Church up-close and to travel with the Cardinal on many occasions including Papal visits. I was deeply honored to serve in this capacity.

The points being made are these: every time I was asked by the Church to do something, I acted like Jeremiah. I thought only of my limitations and weakness. I also wanted to stay where I was most comfortable. Yet, God provided me the grace to say "yes." In doing so, He uplifted, strengthened and sustained me along each and every path. Humility is learning of our complete dependency on God and entrusting our very lives to Him. Our God never disappoints. Our God remains true to His promise that He will be with us always, especially in our time of need. When I was called to serve as Auxiliary Bishop and then as Ordinary of a Diocese, this need for abandonment and surrender repeated itself. I am convinced this "yes" to God's holy will is a life-long and ongoing process.

In addition to walking with God in trust, we must

also realize that we walk with one another. God never wants us to feel alone. As I reflect on the gift of Priesthood, I am ever so thankful for the special people God has placed in my life. I am profoundly grateful for my dear parents, their example of faithful married love, their commitment to family life and their undying support of me and my vocation. I think of my brother Bishops and Priests and the fraternal bond we share. I am so thankful for the Religious who have deeply influenced my life and the lay faithful who have blessed me through their love, prayers and example. There is never a reason to feel alone. God leads us, and we walk together as brothers and sisters.

Sometimes, "walking" is not easy for me. I think of all that must be done in the course of the day. I want to see immediate and visible results. Yet, the Lord often speaks to my heart and tells me to slow down. He reminds me of the need to "walk." I am always reminded of the Gospel story when the Lord sends His disciples out on a journey. He advises them what not take with them: no tunic, walking stick or sandals (Mark 6: 7-11). He is, in essence, telling them not to take anything with them that would weigh them down and keep them from teaching and proclaiming the Good News. He is assuring them that through and in Him and with Him they have everything they need.

What can weigh us down? Anxiety, worry, fear of rejection, need for success and worldly recognition may be a few of these things. Yet, if we trust with profound humility in God's providence, we can slow down. We can walk in serenity. We can be filled with confidence. We can simply give the Lord the best we have to offer and know that He will use it to produce abundant fruit. We can travel lightly, just as the Lord asked His disciples.

It is my hope and prayer that all Priests and those discerning a call to the Priesthood will reflect upon this vocation as gift and mystery, and will be renewed in their trust that the Lord who calls us provides the amazing grace we need. We must keep in mind that our highest priority remains our spiritual lives and our intimate friendship with the Lord, that we must conform ourselves to the mystery of the cross, that our joy is found in our "yes" to His holy will, that God will lead us and that we are assisted by the special people He has placed in our lives. Only then can we travel lightly and walk humbly with our God. Only then can we bring Jesus to others!

Raymond Leo Cardinal Burke

Raymond Leo Cardinal Burke was born in Richland Center, Wisconsin, on June 30, 1948, the youngest of the six children of Thomas F. and Marie B. Burke. His elementary education was undertaken at Saint Mary School in Richland Center (1954-1959) and at Saint Joseph School in Stratford, Wisconsin (1959-1962). He attended high school at Holy Cross Seminary in La Crosse, Wisconsin, from 1962 to 1966, and also completed college courses there (1966 -1968) before attending the Catholic University of America in Washington, D.C., where he studied as a Basselin Scholar (1968-1971). He undertook his studies for ordination at the Pontifical Gregorian University in Rome (1971-1975) and was ordained to the Priesthood by Pope Paul VI on June 29, 1975, at the Basilica of Saint Peter.

Father Burke's first assignment was as associate rector of the Cathedral of Saint Joseph the Workman in La Crosse. In 1977 he took up the additional duty of teaching religion at Aquinas High School in La Crosse. In 1980 Father Burke returned to Rome to study Canon Law at the Pontifical Gregorian University. In April 1984, after completing his studies, he was named Moderator of the Curia and Vice Chancellor of the Diocese of La Crosse.

In 1989 Father Burke returned to Rome when Pope John Paul II named him Defender of the Bond of the Supreme Tribunal of the Apostolic Signatura. After five years in this post, the Holy Father appointed him Bishop of the Diocese of La Crosse on December 10, 1994. Bishop Burke was ordained to the episcopacy by Pope John Paul II on January 6, 1995, at the Basilica of Saint Peter, and was installed in the Diocese of La Crosse on February 22, 1995, the Feast of the Chair of Saint Peter.

On December 2, 2003, Bishop Burke was named Archbishop of Saint Louis. Archbishop Burke was installed in Saint Louis on January 26, 2004, the fifth anniversary of Pope John Paul II's historic pastoral visit to the archdiocese.

On June 27, 2008, His Holiness Pope Benedict XVI appointed Archbishop Burke Prefect of the Supreme Tribunal of the Apostolic Signatura. He also serves on the Congregation for Bishops, the Congregation for Clergy, and the Pontifical Council for Legislative Texts.[1]

---

[1] His Eminence, Raymond Leo Cardinal Burke was elevated to the College of Cardinals on November 20, 2010, after writing his reflection for this anthology.

Priestly Identity and
Devotion to the Sacred Heart of Jesus

Introduction

From my childhood, my parents, parish Priests, and the religious Sisters who taught me in elementary school introduced me to the devotion to the Sacred Heart of Jesus. The image of the Sacred Heart was enthroned in our home, and the observance of the First Friday, the Morning Offering and the invocation of the Sacred Heart throughout the day were quickly learned as habits of prayer. As a child, the devotion seemed to bring into focus all of the various aspects of my life in the Church.

The account of the apparitions of the Sacred Heart of Jesus to Saint Margaret Mary has always strongly attracted me. Each time I read the Promises made to Saint Margaret Mary, I am struck by the immense love of Our Lord Jesus Christ for all men, without boundary.[2] Reflecting upon the Promises has been the occasion for me to continue to deepen my appreciation of the thirst which Christ has for souls, a thirst which truly knows neither measure nor end.

Entering the minor seminary in 1962, I was introduced to the practice of renewing each year the Consecration to the Sacred Heart of Jesus, which was

---

[2] Louis Verheylezoon, S.J., *Devotion to the Sacred Heart of Jesus*, Westminster, Maryland: The Newman Press, 1955, pp. 233-243.

made by Saint Margaret Mary.[3] With the maturing of my Priestly vocation, over the years of seminary formation and the years of my ministry as a Priest and Bishop, the Sacred Heart of Jesus has never ceased to attract me and to draw me into a deeper appreciation of the Sacraments, especially the Sacraments of the Holy Eucharist and Penance, and to a fuller identification of myself with the reality of the Priestly vocation which Saint John Mary Vianney, the Curé of Ars, so simply and powerfully described with these words: "The Priesthood, it is the love of the Heart of Jesus."[4] The devotion to the Sacred Heart of Jesus has kept before my eyes the great wonder of being called to the Priesthood, especially when I have faced temptations to doubt the reality of the Priestly vocation or to treat the reality carelessly or callously.

With these thoughts in mind, I offer some reflections on how the devotion to the Sacred Heart of Jesus has helped me to recognize my Priestly vocation, to embrace the vocation to the Priesthood, and to grow more solidly in my Priestly identity. While other devotions, for example, Eucharistic devotion and devotion to the Blessed Virgin Mary, are an essential

---

3 John Croiset, S.J., *Devotion to the Sacred Heart of Our Lord Jesus Christ*, 2nd ed., tr. Patrick O'Connell, St. Paul, Minnesota: The Radio Replies Press Society, 1959, pp. 242-243.

4 "Le sacerdoce, c'est l'amour du Cœur de Jésus." A. Monnin, *Esprit du Curé d'Ars, Saint J.-B.-M. Vianney dans ses Catéchismes, ses Homélies et sa Conversation*, Paris: Pierre Téqui, 2007, p. 90.

part of the spiritual life of the seminarian and Priest, the devotion to the Sacred Heart of Jesus, in a certain way, draws the whole devotional and prayer life of the seminarian and Priest together in the cultivation of a union of heart with the Heart of Jesus, Head and Shepherd of the flock in every time and place through His ordained Priests. The words of Pope Pius XI, regarding the devotion to the Most Sacred Heart of Jesus, have been verified in my life as both Priest and seminarian:

> [I]s not a summary of all our religion contained in this one devotion? Indeed, it more easily leads our minds to know Christ the Lord intimately and more effectively turns our hearts to love Him more ardently and to imitate Him more perfectly.[5]

What follows are simple reflections. They are certainly not exhaustive but are only meant to point to the substantial enrichment which devotion to the Sacred Heart of Jesus brings to the life of one called to the ordained Priesthood.

---

[5] "[P]ietatis forma nonne totius religionis summa atque adeo perfectioris vitae norma continetur, quippe quae et ad Christum Dominum penitus cognoscendum mentes conducat expeditius et ad eundem vehementius diligendum pressiusque imitandum animos inflectat efficacius?" Pius PP. XI, Litterae Encyclicae, *Miserentissimus Redemptor*, 8 May 1928, *Acta Apostolicae Sedis*, 20 (1928), p. 167.

Recognizing the Priestly Vocation in the Sacred Heart

Growing up in a devout Catholic family, daily prayer with a particular emphasis on the Morning Offering, prayer before and after meals, the Angelus, the Rosary, and night prayer, especially the Examination of Conscience and Act of Contrition; frequent Confession, the Holy Mass, and parish devotions were the heart of my spiritual life. Everything that I learned about my Catholic faith through the teaching of my parents and family members, the Sunday homily of the Priest, and the study of the Catechism naturally led to a fuller and more attentive prayer life, and a singular appreciation of the great reality of the Sacraments as truly actions of Christ alive in the Church for my salvation and the salvation of the world. It was in prayer and through the sacramental life, above all, that I came to know personally the infinite goodness of Christ, which, from my baptism, I have been called to imitate in my thoughts, words and deeds. What impressed me as a child and continues to impress me as an adult is the great richness of our life in the Church, a richness which reflects the ceaseless and immeasurable love with which Christ loves us. Gazing upon the image of the Sacred Heart of Jesus, and having the Sacred Heart of Jesus gaze upon me, I am filled with both the knowledge that our life in the Church is ever new and the desire to know more fully Christ Who is ever giving Himself to us, as if for the first time.

For me, the Sacred Heart of Jesus has always

been the pre-eminent symbol of Christ's love of us in the Church. Having loved us "to the end" by dying for us on the Cross, Christ permitted His heart to be pierced, giving us an unmistakable sign of His unfailing love poured out upon us in the Church from His glorious pierced Heart.[6] It was clear to me as a youngster that the Holy Mass was the greatest gift given to me from the Heart of Jesus. The care with which one prepared for participation in the Holy Mass by the regular confession of sins and even by the simple but significant gesture of dressing in "Sunday clothes" all pointed to Holy Mass and, above all, Holy Communion as the most privileged and most perfect meeting with Christ mysteriously and really present for us in the Church. Serving the Holy Mass, from the time I was in the fourth grade, deepened greatly my appreciation of the greatest mystery of our faith.

Essentially connected to my growing faith in the Holy Eucharist was faith in the Holy Priesthood, the Sacrament by which Christ Himself never fails to make present in the Church the offering of His life for us on the Cross, never fails to make new His Eucharistic Sacrifice. As a child, I was filled with wonder at the Priest who, in the person of Christ, offered the Holy Mass, and heard the confession of my sins and pronounced the words of absolution in the Sacrament of Penance. All of the individual qualities of the various

---

[6] *Jn* 13:1; cf. *Jn* 19:34.

Priests whom I was blessed to know over the years of my childhood and youth were, in the end, not important to me. What stood out was a man given completely to Christ through Priestly ordination.

I think, for instance, of the Priest who first inspired me to consider the vocation to the Priesthood. I was a little boy, and he seemed to me to be an old man, although I know now that he was not, in fact, so very old. He was from Ireland and spoke with a fairly strong accent. Although I did not understand how, I knew, in him, Christ's deep love and care for me. I think, too, of a parish Priest who was beset with a pronounced stutter and how much he inspired me, especially because he struggled so valiantly to teach and preach. I experienced directly the love from the Heart of Jesus in Priests, especially when they were offering the Holy Mass, forgiving my sins in Confession, or hearing my dying father's confession and bringing him Holy Communion.

The devotion to the Sacred Heart of Jesus has helped me over the years to keep focusing on the essence of my life in the Church, namely knowing and loving Christ, and giving myself to Him totally. For that reason, the devotion to the Sacred Heart helped me very much to recognize the call of Christ to follow Him as a true shepherd of the flock. It has kept me focused on the essential place of the Sacraments of the Holy Eucharist and Penance in my daily life, so that Christ could really speak to my heart and draw me to the Holy Priesthood. There can be no question, that the most powerful helps to knowing the vocation to the Priesthood and finding the courage to embrace the vocation are participation in the Holy Mass and prayer before the Most Blessed Sacrament, and frequent access to the Sacrament of Penance.

Through devotion to the Sacred Heart of Jesus, I was helped, in a particular way, to avoid the temptation to envision the Priestly life as a job, a function or a profession in the Church, but, rather, to see the Priesthood as my identity, the identity of Christ the Shepherd, of a man transformed by the mystery of Holy Orders to be truly the love of the Sacred Heart of Jesus for all His brothers and sisters, especially those in most need. In the Sacred Heart of Jesus, I came to understand that Priestly ordination would change my life completely, that Priestly ordination would consecrate every fiber of my being to Christ the High Priest for the sake of His pastoral charity, of His ceaseless and boundless care of the Father's flock.

In that way, during the years of seminary formation, devotion to the Sacred Heart helped me to get over the distraction of particular interests or desires which might have drawn me away from the Priestly vocation. The devotion also helped me to have the conviction and courage that Christ could really be calling me to the Holy Priesthood, and that the love from His Sacred Heart could reach others through me, despite my limitations and weaknesses, if only I would, each day, give my heart completely to Him.

Living the Priestly Vocation in the Sacred Heart of Jesus
Devotion to the Sacred Heart of Jesus has helped me
never to lose sight of the first place which prayer and the
Sacraments must have in my life as a Priest. Entering
into the mystery of the Heart of Jesus, first of all,
uncovers the greatest gifts which flow unceasingly from
His glorious pierced Heart, above all, the gift of His
Body, Blood, Soul and Divinity in the Holy Eucharist.
The Sacred Heart of Jesus indicates to us the
unfathomable mystery of the personal encounter with
Him in the Sacraments and, above all, in the Sacraments
of Penance and the Holy Eucharist. Devotion to the
Sacred Heart of Jesus has kept my liturgical piety
correctly focused on the mystery of the meeting of
Heaven and earth, which takes place at every celebration
of the Sacred Liturgy. Contemplating the mystery of the
love of Christ, symbolized in the Sacred Heart, one hears
addressed to himself the words of Our Lord to Martha:
"Martha, Martha, you are anxious and troubled about
many things, one thing is needful."[7]

Placing my heart anew into the Sacred Heart of
Jesus, I have found a constant help in the battle with
distraction in prayer. In the Heart of Jesus, the
celebration of the Liturgy of the Hours has become more
fully a communion with the universal Church, the whole
Body of Christ, in her ceaseless prayer for the salvation
of the world. While the duties of my life as a Priest may

---

[7] *Lk* 10:41.

not always permit me to pray the Hours at their proper times, throughout the day, the momentary invocation of the mercy of the Heart of Jesus, at the various times of the day, unites me with those in monasteries and other privileged places who are observing the Hours for the sake of us all. The devotion to the Sacred Heart has also confirmed for me the importance of the daily Holy Hour, the treasured time spent simply before the Eucharistic presence of Christ, giving my heart again and, I always hope, more completely, into His Heart.

In His Sacred Heart, Our Lord has also taught me the urgency of the teaching office of the Priest. Our culture is confused or in error about the most fundamental truths, the truth about the inviolable dignity of every human life, about the integrity of marriage and the family, and about the sanctity of conscience. So pervasive is the confusion and error that it has also entered into the life of the Church. The Gospel tells us that, when Our Lord saw the crowds, "he opened his mouth and taught them." [8] It has always been true but is dramatically evident in our time that pastoral charity is first expressed by teaching the faith and the moral life. The very image of the Sacred Heart is one of Christ teaching by showing us His glorious pierced Heart. If I am frequently led to wonder about the loss of faith, for instance, the faith in the Real Presence of Our Lord in the Holy Eucharist, I am reminded of the words

_____

[8] _Mt_ 5:2.

of Saint Paul: "So faith comes from what is heard, and what is heard comes by the preaching of Christ."[9]

It is true that the very confusion and error so prevalent in our culture makes it all the more challenging to teach and preach. There is the temptation to offer pleasing words without offering the solid doctrine which is often difficult to hear, or to remain silent, as if having nothing to say. In reading the Gospels, there is no question that the Heart of God, the Heart of Jesus, is moved with pity for us, and expresses Divine Mercy, first, by teaching us: "As he landed he saw a great throng, and he had compassion on them, because they were like sheep without a shepherd; and he began to teach them many things."[10] From the Heart of Jesus, I have drawn the confidence and the courage to teach and preach; prayer before the image of the Heart of Jesus has often led me to examine my conscience on how well I have announced the Word of Christ through which faith is quickened and given growth. I often think of these words of Saint Paul:

> For if I preach the gospel, that gives me no ground for boasting. For necessity is laid upon me. Woe to me if I do not preach the gospel![11]

---

[9] *Rom* 10:17.

[10] *Mk* 6:34; cf. *Hos* 11:8.

[11] *1 Cor* 9:16.

In the Priestly life, I have also found, in the Heart of Jesus, the courage to speak the truth with love in a culture which prefers "politically correct" language, whether it corresponds to the truth or not, and to live my Catholic faith with integrity in a society whose standard is "getting along", whether it corresponds to the demands of the Catholic faith or not. When I have failed, it is also in the Heart of Jesus that I have found mercy and the courage to begin again on His Way which is Truth and Life. In the Heart of Jesus, I have found the "charity of Christ" which must be the driving force of my Priestly life.[12]

Devotion to the Sacred Heart of Jesus has helped me, in particular, to understand the nature of the call to Priestly celibacy. In the Heart of Jesus, I have found the wisdom and strength to embrace the demands of celibate Priestly love not only as a renunciation of the great good of marriage but as the offering of an undivided heart to the Lord for the shepherding of His flock. To the degree that I have put my Priestly heart into the Sacred Heart of Jesus, my heart has been purified of the selfishness and disordered affections which hinder celibate love, and my heart has been enflamed with pure and selfless love of those entrusted to my Priestly care. In the Heart of Jesus, I have understood that the first and greatest reason for Priestly celibacy is the example of Christ the High Priest to

---

[12] *2 Cor* 5:14.

Whom I have been conformed through the Sacrament of Holy Orders.

Loving others with the Priestly Heart of Jesus is loving them with an undivided heart, a celibate heart. I do not question the purity and greatness of the pastoral love of Priests who are married, but I give testimony to the great gift which the call to celibacy has been for the formation of my Priestly heart. Over the years, I have deepened greatly my appreciation of the discipline of the Latin Church regarding the celibacy of her clergy.[13] I hope to exemplify more and more in my Priestly life the truth of the words with which the Venerable Pope John Paul II described the beauty of the call to Priestly celibacy:

> Celibacy, then, is to be welcomed and continually renewed with a free and loving decision as a priceless gift from God, as an "incentive to pastoral charity", as a singular sharing in God's fatherhood and in the fruitfulness of the Church, and as a witness to the world of the eschatological Kingdom.[14]

---

[13] *Catechism of the Catholic Church*, no. 1579.

[14] "Caelibatus ergo deliberandus est benevolenti ac libera optione, indesinenter renovanda, tanquam inaestimabile Dei donum, velut «stimulus caritatis pastoralis», ut singularis participatio tum in Dei paternitatem tum in Ecclesiae fecunditatem; brevi, ut testimonium mundo exhibitum Regni cuiusdam eschatologici." Ioannes Paulus PP. II, "Adhortatio Apostolica Postsynodalis, *Pastores dabo vobis,*" 25 March 1992, *Acta Apostolicae Sedis*, 84 (1992), p. 705, no. 29.

Devotion to the Sacred Heart of Jesus has uncovered for me, in a particular way, the great beauty of Priestly celibacy and has helped me to verify in my Priestly life the profound meaning of Christ's celibate and Priestly love.

In the Priestly life and ministry, I frequently experience the temptation to be impatient with members of the flock in my care or with the flock, in general. Often enough, too, the pastoral needs of the faithful do not coincide with the plans which I have made or the schedule that I have devised. In other words, the call for my Priestly ministration is frequently not convenient for me. I also suffer the temptation to discount the importance of taking extra care with my teaching and preaching, or with my celebrating of the Holy Mass and the other sacred rites, or with my giving pastoral counsel and direction, doubting that the extra attention I give to sacred offices will really make a difference for those whom I am called to be a true shepherd. There is also the temptation to ruminate on the inadequacies with which I have fulfilled the office of pastoral charity in the past, whether in teaching, or celebrating the Sacraments, or giving pastoral direction and administering the Church's discipline, and, as a result, to become discouraged.

Uniting my Priestly heart to the Sacred Heart of Christ the High Priest, I have discovered resources of patience which I never imagined that I could have. Christ invites Priests, in a most particular way, to accept the yoke of His love and to learn from Him Who is, in His own words, "gentle and lowly in heart," and to find in Him alone "rest for [their] souls."[15] To the degree that I can give my heart to Christ, He exercises through me that remarkable patience with sin, incomprehension and hardness of heart, which He unfailingly manifested during His public ministry. His thirst for souls, which is learned in His Eucharistic Heart, overcomes any human inclination to be short with or to dismiss any soul. I think, for instance, of His prayer for the forgiveness of those who were the ministers of His cruel Passion and Death: "Father, forgive them; for they know not what they do."[16] In the Sacred Heart of Jesus, I have also found the energy to respond to the unexpected demands upon my Priestly heart which I had thought to have exhausted, for the moment, its resources of love.

In the Sacred Heart of Jesus, I have also come to a deeper understanding of my Priestly vocation as spiritual fatherhood. I have come to understand that the renunciation of the good of marriage is not the renunciation of my manhood but rather the giving of my distinct gifts as a man to Christ, so that He can be Head and Shepherd of the flock. In the Heart of Jesus, I have come to know both the tenderness of the love of the Shepherd and also its steadfastness. In the Heart of Jesus, I have learned the importance of the guidance

---

[15] *Mt* 11:29.

[16] *Lk* 23:34.

and correction which are an essential part of loving the flock. "For the Lord disciplines him whom he loves, and chastises every son whom he receives."[17]

When the demands of the Priestly ministry have seemed too great for me, or I have been tempted to the vice of self-pity, devotion to the Sacred Heart of Jesus has helped me to reflect upon the unconditional love of a father for his children. In this regard, the friendship of families has meant so much to me as a Priest. Witnessing the unconditional love of husband and wife for each other, and for their children has inspired in me the same unconditional love for the souls placed in my Priestly care. When I have been called out in the middle of the night to minister to the sick and dying, or am called to give extended time to a soul going through particular troubles, I think of parents who get up so often in the night to care for an infant or a sick child, and who give countless hours to a child, young or old, who is in trouble. At the same time, the couples with whom I have become a close friend, over the years, have often expressed to me what inspiration and strength they draw from knowing more deeply the heart of a Priest.

Conclusion

Finally, devotion to the Sacred Heart of Jesus has led me to an intimate spiritual bond with the Blessed Virgin

_____

[17] *Heb* 12:6; cf. *Dt* 8:5.

Mary, the Mother of Jesus, under whose Immaculate Heart, as the Venerable Pope John Paul II reminded us, God the Son took a human heart, and with the whole company of saints. The Blessed Virgin Mary, in her maternal love, has drawn me to her Immaculate Heart, so that she might lead me to the Heart of her Son, as she led the wine stewards at the Wedding Feast of Cana to Jesus with the instruction: "Do whatever he tells you."[18] Through her message and apparitions, under the title of Our Lady of Guadalupe, a title which is particularly dear to Priests of the continent of America, she had led me into an ever deeper understanding of the mercy and love of God, made flesh for us in her Divine Son.

The saints have taught me the many and rich dimensions of the mystery of Divine Mercy and Love, symbolized in the Sacred Heart of Jesus. So many saints, my own patron saints, the patron saints of the places in which I have served as a Priest and Bishop, the Priest saints, like Saint John Mary Vianney and Saint Maximilian Kolbe; the great doctors of the Church, those saints who helped me greatly in the spiritual life, like Saint Thérèse of Lisieux and Saint Faustina Kowalska, and many others have helped me and continue to help me to be "the love of the Heart of Jesus."

As a Priest, I have wanted to be with Mary at the foot of the Cross, as Saint John the Apostle and Evangelist was, and to lift up my heart, with her

---

[18] *Jn* 2:5.

Immaculate Heart, to the pierced Heart of Jesus. With Mary, I have wanted to bear my portion of the burden of the sufferings of Christ for the sake of the salvation of all. I sincerely want to be able to say with Saint Paul:

> Now I rejoice in my sufferings for your sake, and in my flesh I complete what is lacking in Christ's afflictions for the sake of his body, that is, the church, of which I became a minister according to the divine office which was given to me for you, to make the word of God fully known, the mystery hidden for ages and generations but now made manifest to his saints.[19]

I have sensed Mary's unfailing company, giving example and encouragement, and interceding for so many graces, throughout my years in the seminary and in the Priestly ministry, especially in the times when I have been severely tried and tempted. I have sensed, too, the help of so many saints, especially my patron saints, all one with me in the Heart of Jesus.

It is my hope that these reflections express, in some small way, my profound gratitude to God our Father for the call to the ordained Priesthood, the vocation to be "the love of the Heart of Jesus," His only-begotten Son, for the salvation of my brothers and sisters, and of our world. The reality of the ordained Priesthood is indeed a mystery beyond all our comprehending. The saintly Curé of Ars reminds us that

---

[19] *Col* 1:24-26.

the Priest will only comprehend the greatness of the Priesthood in heaven, declaring: "If one would understand it on earth, he would die not of fright but of love." [20] It is my prayer that seminarians and Priests who read these simple and poor reflections may be inspired, through the devotion to the Sacred Heart of Jesus, to an ever deeper understanding of the great reality of the Priesthood and thereby to a more ardent love of Christ, in Whose very person, they are called to shepherd the Father's flock.

+ Raymond Leo Burke
Archbishop Emeritus of Saint Louis
Prefect of the Supreme Tribunal of the Apostolic Signatura
11 June 2010 – Solemnity of the Most Sacred Heart of Jesus

---

[20] "Si on le comprenait sur la terre, on mourrait non de frayeur mais d'amour." A. Monnin, *Esprit du Curé d'Ars, Saint J.-B.-M. Vianney dans ses Catéchismes, ses Homélies et sa Conversation*, Paris: Pierre Téqui, 2007, p. 87.

FATHER GREGORY FAIRBANKS

Rev. Gregory J Fairbanks is the youngest of five children of Richard and Dorothy Fairbanks. Raised in Plymouth Meeting, PA, he attended his parish elementary school, Epiphany of our Lord, and then Bishop Kenrick High School. After high school he attended Villanova University where he earned a BA in Economics, with minors in History and Religious Studies. Upon graduation from Villanova, he entered Saint Charles Borromeo Seminary for the Archdiocese of Philadelphia. Ordained in 1990, his Priestly assignments have included Christ the King Parish in Philadelphia, Temple University Newman Center, post-graduate studies in Church History at the Gregorian University in Rome, Professor of Church History at Saint Charles Borromeo Seminary and Director of the Office of Ecumenical and Interreligious Affairs. Since 2008 he has served as an Official of the Pontifical Council for Promoting Christianity in the Vatican.

Reconciliation Is a Key
to the Mission of the Church

What does it mean to be a Priest? It is a simple question, but one in which the answer is full of unexpected twists and turns. Having been involved in various Priestly ministries in the Church, I must honestly state that if someone were to ask me what I would be doing today twenty-five years ago when I entered the seminary, I never would have guessed my current ministry. Then again, I would not have guessed several of the different assignments I have had in my twenty years as a Priest. Twenty five years ago when I applied to seminary, during my entrance interview, the seminary officials asked me why I was applying to the seminary. My response was that the Priesthood had been something I had been thinking about for many years, at least back to early high school, and I wanted to see if it was my calling. I stated that I did not want to wake up when I was 60 years old (which seemed like an eternity away back then) and think, "I wonder if I should have tried the seminary?" I wanted to be closer to God, and being a Priest was where I felt God was calling me. The seminary would be the place to discern that call.

As time went on, I came to appreciate all the more that being a Priest was about bringing the sacraments to people and to preach the Gospel. I imagined that I would be a parish Priest, baptizing children, witnessing marriages, bringing the sacraments to the sick, comforting the families of the deceased, and leading people in prayer. These are things I do as a Priest. Yet, I have also done other things as a Priest. As I reflect now for this book, why I answered the call to be a Priest was not so much in the doing of Priestly ministry (although that is important!), but even more the philosophical sense of 'being' a Priest – Priestly identity. These elements are still only parts of the answer to that question 25 years ago. At a basic level, I believe I chose to enter seminary for a much simpler reason. I wanted to have my life make a difference. There are so many times a Priest makes a difference in people's lives.

In my first Priestly assignment, I was an associate in a mid-sized parish in Northeast Philadelphia, Christ the King. It was an assignment of eight wonderful years. Those times included baptisms – welcoming with joy new Christians into the Church, the Rite of Christian Initiation of Adults (RCIA) – welcoming adults into the Catholic Church, weddings – celebrating the love and new life in the vocation of marriage, and funerals – praying with a family when the family is saying farewell to a loved one in the joy and hope of eternal life. The parish also served as chaplains to a hospital with a trauma center, so hospital ministry was an important part of my first 8 years as a Priest. It was a rare week that I was not awakened at least once (usually several) times at night for a hospital call.

That ministry taught me a lot about Priestly identity. The call in the middle of the night was not for Gregory Fairbanks, but for 'Father'. I brought the sacrament of the sick to the dying. I heard final confessions. If possible, I gave last Eucharist. It was not about me, but what I am. I am a Priest. It is the sacraments, the presence of Jesus, that I brought. With that presence, that of Jesus Christ, I brought peace, reconciliation, and calm to very frightening and trying moments in peoples lives. Not just the sick person, but to their family and friends as well. I was a vehicle for the Lord to work through me. It is He who is the minister, the High Priest.

As a young Priest, I was asked to be the coordinator for ecumenical (intra-Christian) and interreligious (relations with non-Christians) affairs in the territorial vicariate of the parish where I was stationed. I accepted the invitation, and began to learn in a new way how to engage with other Christians and non-Christians. In the beginning, my engagement was mostly with various Protestant denominations and with the local Jewish community. Later did relations with Muslims and other religions slowly increase, as the religious mix of the Philadelphia area changed. Along with the various levels of theological and social action engagements, our local ministerium of Christian leaders became affectionately known as the 'Perkins Ministerium'. Once a month, we would hold a lunch meeting at a local Perkins restaurant and plan the various events that the ministerium would sponsor, such as the annual prayer service for Christian Unity Week. It was also a time for Christian pastors to come together to share the ups and downs of ministry, the difficulties and successes we each encounter, and to confer with each other about our neighborhood concerns. By coming together and becoming friends, we realized how much we have in common, while being honest about our differences. In the informal gathering of a common meal, we shared the joys and frustrations of ministry, as well as finding out how our ecclesiology's manifest themselves at the parish level. While some of us were assigned to our parishes, others had sought out their 'call', the local parish church. When a marriage would take place between our parishioners, it was much easier when we as pastors could show how we can work together while maintaining our beliefs. When a funeral would affect an interchurch family, the healing of Priest and minster at the funeral together, each in our respective roles depending on the community, showed the bond of compassion and faith and hope for eternal life that we all share.

Later on I directed the Philadelphia Archdiocesan Office for Ecumenical and Interreligious Affairs. It was an honor to be a part of the formation of the Religious Leaders Council of Greater Philadelphia. This new body of the heads of Christian, Jewish and Muslim communities took on the prophetic role of reconciliation in the local community. With the head leadership of

Catholic (Latin and Ukrainian), Orthodox, Protestants, Jews and Muslims, which included Bishops, conference ministers, rabbis and imams, the religious leaders stood together in a common witness of the faith community. In addition to the top leadership level, an executive committee worked with our respective religious leaders to deepen the relationships among the varied faith communities in the local area. We tried to not only be a witness to the wider community, but also to build up relationships between our communities. At the parish level, the most often heard reservation to working with people from other churches/mosques/synagogues is that 'we' need to keep 'our own people' in our churches/mosques/synagogues – and not to try and have our people become 'confused'. This was a view held by many – not just Catholics. I can honestly state that when people, whether in ministry or 'in the pews', begin to talk and work together with other believers that each person goes home strengthened in their own faith. The personal relationships formed in the Religious Leaders Council helped immensely when a tragic series of deaths of Philadelphia Police officers began. The Religious Leaders were able to stand together and pray alongside each other during the funerals and reconciliation services. Had the personal relationships formed in the Religious Leaders Council not been in place, the common witness of the faith community in times of tragedy could have been awkward.

Currently, my ministry assignment is in Rome at the Pontifical Council for Promoting Christian Unity (PCPCU). The PCPCU has two principal foci, first it is entrusted with the promotion, within the Catholic Church, of an authentic ecumenical spirit according to the Vatican II decree on ecumenism, *Unitatis Redintegratio,* and secondly it aims to develop dialogue and collaboration with other Churches and World Communions. The principal areas of my responsibility includes relations with Reformed Christians (spiritual heirs to John Calvin), Anabaptists, and the Faith and Order Commission of the World Council of Churches. With each of these groups, I interact with staff counterparts with the respective groups, and with the theologian experts each team assembles. The PCPCU also relates to local Catholic dioceses and Episcopal Conferences, such as the United States Conference of Catholic Bishops, on ecumenical matters. Much of the ecumenical journey, locally and internationally, is about relationships. Only with an attitude and atmosphere of trust can true dialogue take place.

The first steps in dialogue are usually about definition of terms and a common understanding of history. Historical memories, of which we often are not consciously aware, shape our mindsets in discerning the present. Too often we have taught about each other from our own tradition's historical memory and viewpoint, while not asking the 'other' what they actually do teach and believe. For instance, the word 'Reformation' is in itself both a term and an evaluation of the 16th century. We may not think of it consciously that way, but classical Catholic theology would never have used that term to describe the emergent Protestant communities of the 16th century. The word 'Reformation' itself has entered our vocabulary, especially in 'Protestant' majority countries. One of the tasks of the ecumenical movement is to as objectively as possible study the roots of Christian division, so that we can move more effectively to the ultimate level of ecumenism, which is the goal of full visible unity of Christians. That ultimate goal of ecumenism, full visible unity, is the end goal of the ecumenical movement. It is the stated goal of the World Council of Churches and of the Catholic Church. Jesus desired that his disciples 'be one.. so that the world may believe' (John 17). With this Scriptural understanding, division among Christians is against the will of Christ, and it is therefore incumbent on Christians to try and heal those divisions. The Priest, as a minister of reconciliation, has the challenge to bring his reconciling and healing ministry to the wider level of communities of faith to heal and reconcile division among Christians.

In 1910 there was the First World Missionary Conference in Edinburgh, Scotland. With the danger of being overly simplistic about the Conference, it was a meeting of mostly British Isles Protestants who realized that in their missionary activity in un-evangelized areas (especially in Africa), was being hurt by the divisions in

Christianity. By bringing the European Protestant divisions to the mission territories, they were in fact hindering evangelization. People who did not know Christ did not need to be sure to be Scottish Presbyterians as opposed to Dutch Reformed, or any other imported divisions. The World Missionary Conference is considered to be the birth of the modern ecumenical movement. This mission movement joined with another theological commission (Faith and Order) after World War II to form the World Council of Churches. The important realization in the modern ecumenical movement was that *division among* Christians is a poor *witness to* non-Christians about the faith. The link between mission and ecumenism was beginning to be understood.

One example of how ecumenism works and can be effective came during recent Baptist-Catholic International Theological Conversations. As a Catholic Priest, devotion to Our Lady is an important part of my spirituality. During one of the meetings, our conversations on Mary was particularly interesting. With Protestants in the tradition of John Calvin (Baptists have an historical rooting in a mixture of Reformed and Anabaptist theology), Catholic devotion to Mary is one of the greatest cultural divides between Catholics and Protestants. Other theological divides are also significant. The difference in individual Baptists approaches reflect the particular culture from which they came. Latin American Baptists, living in an overwhelmingly 'Catholic' context, have a different experience and view than African Baptists who came from a relatively 'newly Christianized' context. The European and North American Baptists have the centuries old historicity of the Reformation era disputes. Catholics on the dialogue also had different emphases in their approach due to their own cultural approaches. Reconciling can be a challenge on a personal level, as well as in intellectual discussions. This challenge cuts both ways, for me as a Catholic with Marian devotion as an important part of my spirituality, and for some Baptists who associate Marian devotion with idolatry.

The reason I mention the discussions on Mary within the context of ecumenical dialogue and the hopes for the future, is because I believe this point exemplifies one way ecumenism works. The PCPCU has about 20 active dialogues with various Christian communions. Each one has its own context and story. As one might imagine, dialogue with the Baptists is different than dialogue with the Eastern Orthodox. The issues, history, and context are all very different. Much of the theological divide has to do with culture, especially cultural memories. Reconciliation is a key to the mission of the Church.

The work of Christian unity involves being faithful to the truth of the Church's teaching. The PCPCU in its *Directory for the Application and Norms on Ecumenism* clearly states that: "In our day there exists here and there a certain tendency to doctrinal confusion. Also it is very important in the ecumenical sphere, as in other spheres, to avoid abuses which could either contribute to or entail doctrinal indifferentism."[21] This is part of the challenge for Christian unity, to differentiate what issues are of 'truth', from what is legitimate diversity of expression and practice. No matter what the historical context of past division, who and where the present dialogue partners come from, the first level of ecumenism is the cornerstone on which all other dialogue is built: to accurately understand what each Christian denomination actually teaches and believes. Understanding the context and history of division is paramount for eventual reconciliation. Too often we tend to teach our communities *our* history, and the history of the 'other,' through the prism of *our* historical memory. We certainly do not advocate a model of 'political anarchy' which suggests that all history must be destroyed in order to build a new untainted future. Instead, one of the greatest gifts that the ecumenical movement has achieved, since generations of dialogue have studied in varied details, is a fresh look together at our common history of division, rather than only through our own historical prisms. This work has been done in large part, but is scattered throughout the tomes of ecumenical dialogue texts, usually labelled as 'the healing of memories.' The

---

[21] DIRECTORY FOR THE APPLICATION OF PRINCIPLES AND NORMS ON ECUMENISM, §6.

healing of memories sections were usually done as early ecumenical dialogue studies with each tradition. The goal was to look at the roots of division, as well as persecutions of the 'other,' from an historical and non-polemical point of view.

I believe that the ecumenical movement has had a greater effect than most people realize. It is taken for granted that different Christian communions dialogue with each other. That was not the case 50 years ago. Ministerium meetings between clergy of the denominations are common events today. This was not so 50 years ago. This is not reflective of a tendency to doctrinal confusion, but part of an honest exchange of beliefs with pastoral sensitivity.

People desire unity in a way that was unthought-of a few generations ago. The effect of these trends cannot be underestimated. We have each in our ways rediscovered that what we emphasised to show our denominational identity could be maintained while still being open to the gifts of the other. Catholics have opened themselves up in greater ways to the Scriptures. Protestants have begun to reemphasize the sacraments. The saints, and Mary in particular, have begun to be appreciated by some Protestants. Enriching the Liturgy of the Word, Catholics regularly engage in the prayerful reading of scripture in *lectio divina*. The practice of *lectio divina* is now shared by both Catholics and Protestants.

Back to the Baptist-Catholic dialogue: Catholics and Baptists listening to each about Marian devotion helps each side to understand their point of view. Some Baptists hold their resistance to Marian devotion as an integral part of Baptist identity. Some Catholics in practice seem to emphasize Mary even more than Christ, though that is not their intent. Getting over the 'gut level' feelings of identity and division is a work of conversion of our own hearts. What is important is not that 'I am right,' but that the *right thing is believed*. Some issues are a matter of right and wrong. Some issues just have different emphases. The key is know the difference between the two, to identify what truly belongs to the Body of Christ, the Church. It is all part of the process of reconciling people and communities.

The courage to view history through the eyes of the other is the first step towards unity. That courage needs conversion of hearts. By opening our hearts to conversion, we can look at our own history in the eye without fear. One thing is sure, only by each Christian opening their hearts to conversion can we grow in faith, and only then can growth in unity be achieved. Vatican II's decree on ecumenism put it this way:

> "All the faithful should remember that the more effort they make to live holier lives according to the Gospel, the better will they further Christian unity and put it into practice. For the closer their union with the Father, the Word, and the Spirit, the more deeply and

easily will they be able to grow in mutual brotherly love." *UR 7*

The Priest involved in the work of Christian unity must always be mindful that it is not his work, but the work of the Holy Spirit. We have come a long way on what will be long journey. If we truly believe that the prayer of Jesus is true, "that they all may be one; even as you, Father, are in me, and I in you, that they also may be one in us, so that the world may believe that you have sent me." (Jn 17) we have no choice but to continue to do our part in the reconciliation that only He can work. This work is for all Christians. For some it is to be in active ecumenical endeavors. For all of us it is a call to share in the prayer of Jesus with our own prayers for unity. The work is not of our own doing, but the work of Christ in His Spirit. In this sense, the ministry of Christian unity is yet another example of living out a Priestly identity. It is a way of letting ourselves become vehicles for Christ to work in and though us. It is a way to bring peace and reconciliation to the world. It is a way to make a difference, even if only in a small way. God does have mysterious ways of guiding our lives. This may not be what I imagined I would be doing 25 years ago, but it is an answer of serving the Church as Christ wills. That is what it means to be a Priest.

John Patrick Cardinal Foley

John Patrick Cardinal Foley, Grand Master of the Equestrian Order of the Holy Sepulchre of Jerusalem, was born on November 11, 1935 in Darby, Pennsylvania.

After earning a bachelor's degree in history and in philosophy, he was ordained a Priest on May 19, 1962. He then became assistant pastor at Sacred Heart Church in Philadelphia. In 1963, he was named assistant editor of The Catholic Standard and Times, and while he went to Rome to continue his studies, he served as Rome correspondent.

In 1965 he received a doctorate in philosophy from the University of Saint Thomas Aquinas in Rome and then in 1966 a Master of Science in Journalism from Columbia University. In 1967, he returned to The Catholic Standard and Times as assistant editor and was professor of philosophy at Saint Charles Borromeo Seminary, Philadelphia.

From 1966 until 1974, he was co-producer and co-host of the Philadelphia Catholic Hour on the local radio. He was also co-producer of the television series "The Making of a Priest" for Group W Television in the United States, and was active in other radio and television productions.

In 1970 he was named editor of The Catholic Standard and Times. A position he held until 1984. In

1976, he was named an honorary prelate of His Holiness.

He served as news secretary for the meetings of the National Conference of Catholic Bishops in the United States and as English-language press liaison for the visit of Pope John Paul II to Ireland and the United States in 1979 and for the Synod of Bishops in Rome in 1980.

On April 9, 1984 he was appointed president of the Pontifical Commission (now Pontifical Council) for Social Communications and titular Archbishop of Neapolis in Proconsulari. He was ordained a Bishop on May 8, 1984. From August that year until 1989, he was president of the administrative council of the Vatican Television Centre. He also founded the Vatican's film library.

On June 27, 2007 Pope Benedict XVI appointed him Pro-Grand Master of the Equestrian Order of the Holy Sepulchre of Jerusalem, and on December 22, 2007 he became Grand Master. He was created and proclaimed Cardinal by Benedict XVI in the consistory of November 24, 2007, of the Deaconry of San Sebastiano al Palatino (Saint Sebastian on the Palatine).

Enthronement of the Heart of Jesus

When I was a newly ordained Priest, I was providentially assigned to Sacred Heart Church in Haverford Township in suburban Philadelphia. The pastor, Father Thomas B. Falls, had been my professor of patrology at Saint Charles Borromeo Seminary in Philadelphia and he was also the chaplain for the Philadelphia Senatus of the Legion of Mary, a jurisdiction which took in the entire Commonwealth of Pennsylvania.

Father Falls (he later became a Monsignor and was one of the four pastor observers from the United States at the Second Vatican Council) had suggested to the parish praesidium of the Legion of Mary that they ask during their house-to-house visitations of parishioners how many families would want to have the Enthronement of the Sacred Heart in their homes.

The response was overwhelming and, as the newly ordained assistant pastor, I was given the task of visiting all the families who wished to have the Enthronement.

In most homes, the ceremony was very simple – a blessing of an image of the Sacred Heart and the recitation of an Act of Contrition. Some invited the neighbors and had a modest party after the ceremony – after all, they did live in Sacred Heart parish! Some used the visit of the Priest as an opportunity to bring some long neglected problems to the surface – especially the problem of a lack of canonical form of marriage.

In one case, where there was the danger of death of one party in an invalid marriage after divorce, permission was obtained for fraternal cohabitation so that the couple could join their children in receiving the Eucharist.

In another case, a *sanatio in radice* ("healing at the root" – a recognition by the Church of enduring consent when a non–Catholic party is unwilling to renew consent in the Catholic Church) was obtained so that the Catholic party could return to the Sacraments. In those days the chancery office assigned a penance to the Catholic party for any scandal which had been given – and the penance in this case was the recitation of the Rosary every day for a month. Years later I returned to the parish after I had been named a Bishop, and the man who had received the penance came up to me and asked if I remembered him and the penance he had been given. When I said that I did, he replied that he had said the Rosary every day for a month and that he said the Rosary every day since then – and that he had offered it for me! He died shortly after that, but his non–Catholic wife continued to assist at Mass every Sunday without ever entering the Church!

Other visits for the Enthronement of the Sacred Heart were less dramatic but not less inspiring. After almost fifty years, I still hear from some of the families in whose homes the Sacred Heart was enthroned, and they report that they are still reciting their family prayers of devotion to the Sacred Heart every evening!

As a college student, I remember having read the life of Saint Margaret Mary Alacoque and of the apparitions of Our Lord to her and of the promises He made for devotion to His Sacred Heart. The one which I most treasure as a Priest is: "I will give to Priests the power to touch the most hardened hearts."

Because of the confidentiality of the confessional, I cannot enter into details about how I have seen this promise verified – but it has been, and I have been inspired and am deeply grateful that the "Love of the Heart of Jesus" has played such a special role in my own Priestly life.

BISHOP PAUL S. LOVERDE

Bishop Loverde was ordained a Priest for service in the Diocese of Norwich on December 18, 1965, in the Basilica of Saint Peter in Rome. He served in a variety of assignments both on the parochial and diocesan levels. In 1988 he was ordained an Auxiliary Bishop for the Archdiocese of Hartford, was installed as the eleventh Bishop of Ogdensburg, New York in 1994, and became the third Bishop of Arlington in 1999.

He served as Chairman of the Bishops' Committee on Vocations from 1995 to 1998, and was a member of the Bishops' Administrative Committee from 2004 to 2008. In addition to being the Chair of the Board of Trustees at CDU, he is a member of the Board of Trustees of the Catholic University of America. He also is a member of the Board of Directors of The Institute for Psychological Sciences.

A Determined Witness to the Gospel:
The Evangelical Counsels in Priestly Life

In his June 16, 2009 *Letter Proclaiming a Year for Priests*, Pope Benedict XVI wrote:

> In today's world, as in the troubled times of the Curé of Ars, the lives and activity of Priests need to be distinguished by *a determined witness to the Gospel*. As Pope Paul VI rightly noted, 'modern man listens more willingly to witnesses than to teachers, and if he does listen to teachers, it is because they are witnesses'. Lest we experience existential emptiness and the effectiveness of our ministry be compromised, we need to ask ourselves ever anew: 'Are we truly pervaded by the word of God? Is that word truly the nourishment we live by, even more than bread and the things of this world? Do we really know that word? Do we love it? Are we deeply engaged with this word to the point that it really leaves a mark on our lives and shapes our thinking?' Just as Jesus called the Twelve to be with him (cf. Mk 3:14), and only later sent them forth to preach, so too in our days Priests are called to assimilate that 'new style of life' which was inaugurated by the Lord Jesus and taken up by the Apostles.

What is this "new style of life," of which Pope Benedict speaks, that will distinguish the Priest as "a determined witness to the Gospel"?

Blessed Pope John XXIII, in his 1959 Encyclical Letter *Sacerdotii nostri primordia*, published on the first centenary of the death of Saint John Mary Vianney,

71

the patron saint of parish Priests, referred to "three evangelical counsels" as distinguishing signs of Saint John Vianney's witness of life. I submit that *understanding and living* these three evangelical counsels is what will constitute a new lifestyle as a determined witness to the Gospel. "It was complete commitment to this 'new style of life' which marked the Priestly ministry of the Curé of Ars. Pope John XXIII... presented his asceticism with special reference to the 'three evangelical counsels' which the Pope considered necessary also for diocesan Priests: 'even though Priests are not bound to embrace these evangelical counsels by virtue of the clerical state, these counsels nonetheless offer them, as they do all the faithful, the surest road to the desired goal of Christian perfection'. The Curé of Ars lived the 'evangelical counsels' in a way suited to his Priestly state".[22]

I would like to reflect on these three evangelical counsels exemplified in the life of Saint John Vianney, so that in turn we may learn how to live them ourselves, not only during this Year for Priests, but for the rest of our lives as Priests witnessing to the Gospel and reflecting the love of the Heart of Jesus.

---

[22] Pope Benedict XVI, *Letter Proclaiming a Year for Priests*, 16 June 2009.

Poverty

"His *poverty* was not the poverty of a religious or a monk, but that proper to a Priest: while managing much money (since well-to-do pilgrims naturally took an interest in his charitable works), he realized that everything had been donated to his church, his poor, his orphans, the girls of his '*Providence*', his families of modest means. Consequently, he 'was rich in giving to others and very poor for himself'.[23] As he would explain: 'My secret is simple: give everything away; hold nothing back'. When he lacked money, he would say amiably to the poor who knocked at his door: 'Today I'm poor just like you, I'm one of you'. At the end of his life, he could say with absolute tranquility: 'I no longer have anything. The good Lord can call me whenever he wants!'".[24]

What does living the evangelical counsel of poverty mean in the life of a diocesan Priest? It means a truly simple life style. Let us examine *how* we live. Do we have a *habitual* preference for the best in food, drink, clothing, furnishings, automobiles, gadgets? *Habitual* is the key. Now and again we can enjoy a special meal, a fine suit, a special item, but with an attitude that does not place me in the center: "I'm a Priest, so I'm special and I want to be treated as such. I'm entitled...." For

---

[23] http://www.vatican.va/holy_father/benedict_xvi/letters/2009/documents/hf_ben-xvi_let_20090616_anno-sacerdotale_en.html -_ftn37#_ftn37

[24] Pope Benedict XVI, *Letter Proclaiming a Year for Priests*, 16 June 2009.

example, do we expect preferred seating in restaurants? Do we seek special discounts? Are we unwilling to be inconvenienced? While respecting our need for adequate rest, sufficient exercise, time away in order to be re-created, are we available to God and to His people, especially those in need? Yes, the doorbell and the telephone and now the e-mails, texting, etc., can be annoying, invading, "a real pain." But is it *about us* or is it about Him and them? Can we leave the Christ Who encounters us in prayer in order to respond to Christ Who encounters us in that unexpected call, or office visit, or hospital visit? At the same time we need to avoid extremes – never taking time for oneself or taking an inordinate amount of time for oneself.

Our poverty lies in our willingness to be available to others, to give the gift of our time and of our very selves for their sake whether they deserve it or not, whether they refuse the invitation or not! Our poverty also lies in our admission of our radical dependence on the Lord: "Without me, you can do nothing" (cf. Jn. 15:5).

Do we really go to the Lord in our radical need for His grace-filled assistance? Especially in situations which seem impossible for us to resolve on our own? Are we poor in spirit: "Blessed are those who know their need for God" (cf. Mt. 5:3)?

Chastity

"His *chastity*, too, was that demanded of a Priest for his ministry. It could be said that it was a chastity suited to one who must daily touch the Eucharist, who contemplates it blissfully and with that same bliss offers it to his flock. It was said of him that 'he radiated chastity'; the faithful would see this when he turned and gazed at the tabernacle with loving eyes".[25] We are called to be *chaste and celibate – both* are *required* and *expected*. Our beloved is the Lord Jesus – and only the Lord Jesus. Our celibate chastity forms the "stuff of spousal love" enabling us to give ourselves wholly to Christ, conforming ourselves to Him in His nuptial union with His Bride, the Church. Are we celibate? Are we chaste? Are we aware of our own humanity, with its weaknesses and proneness to seeking one's pleasures? If the goal is to make Jesus the love of our hearts, to love Him above all others, to respond to His desire to draw us into real intimacy with Him, then, everything we think, say and *especially do* must be in harmony with that goal, in support of that goal. We must be aware of and resist or break off relationships and situations that begin *eroding the goal*. Friendships are integral to our well-being: Priestly friendships and lay friendships. Friendship, however, can begin *to be more*, i.e., an emotional bond with subsequent *needs*. In this area,

---

[25] Pope Benedict XVI, *Letter Proclaiming a Year for Priests*, 16 June 2009.

perhaps above all, we need to be honest and realistic. For example, just having lunch or dinner with one person can be "official" or "professional" – once or twice. But more frequent occasions can often send up yellow flags. Let me give another example: we'll have drinks at her home – her husband is away and the children are asleep. Drinks can lead to a friendly hug – then perhaps a little more than a friendly hug. We must be realistic! If we fire up dynamite, why should we be surprised when it explodes?

As Priests committed to chaste celibate living, we are called to exercise discernment in our friendships. Are the relationships in our lives helping, fostering, and deepening our intimacy with Jesus, or are they weakening, eroding, even destroying it? Can we bring our friendships to Jesus, look Him straight in the eye and ask Him to bless them?

On their wedding day, husbands and wives make vows to each other: "I will be true to you in good times and in bad, in sickness and in health, all the days of my life." So too do we promise Christ and His Church that we will be true and faithful, in good times and in bad, in sickness and in health all the days of our lives. Surely in the life of every Priest there will be lonely times – are we willing to bring them to Jesus, to bring ourselves to Jesus, and find in Him our hearts' desire?

Obedience

"Finally, Saint John Mary Vianney's *obedience* found full embodiment in his conscientious fidelity to the daily demands of his ministry. We know how he was tormented by the thought of his inadequacy for parish ministry and by a desire to flee 'in order to bewail his poor life, in solitude'. Only obedience and a thirst for souls convinced him to remain at his post. As he explained to himself and his flock: 'There are no two good ways of serving God. There is only one: serve him as he desires to be served'.[26] He considered this the golden rule for a life of obedience: 'Do only what can be offered to the good Lord'".[27]

The root of the word "obedience" is "*ob-audire*" – "to listen." Ultimately, obedience involves listening to the Lord. He speaks through those He has appointed to oversee us: the Pope for the Bishops; Bishops for Priests; and religious superiors for religious Priests. Obedience presumes an attitude. Whose? Christ's. And what was His attitude? "Have among yourselves the same attitude that is also yours in Christ Jesus, Who, though he was in the form of God, did not regard equality with God something to be grasped. Rather, he emptied himself, taking the form of a slave, coming in human likeness;

---

[26] http://www.vatican.va/holy_father/benedict_xvi/letters/2009/documents/hf_ben-xvi_let_20090616_anno-sacerdotale_en.html -_ftn43#_ftn43

[27] Pope Benedict XVI, *Letter Proclaiming a Year for Priests*, 16 June 2009.

and found human in appearance, he humbled himself, becoming obedient to death, even death on a cross. Because of this, God greatly exalted him and bestowed on him the name that is above every name, that at the name of Jesus every knee should bend, of those in heaven and on earth and under the earth, and every tongue confess that Jesus Christ is Lord, to the glory of God the Father" (Phil 2:5-11). In a word, Christ's obedience expressed itself in His act of *kenosis*, i.e., self-emptying in accord with God the Father's will. Jesus said: "I have come to do Your Will" (Heb. 10:9). Jesus did His Father's will His whole life long, especially in the Agony in the Garden and with the Cross He bore.

The virtue of obedience enables us, especially as Priests, to adopt Christ's attitude, the essential attitude, the only one, for us His disciples, the people who belong to Him. When we face difficulties, trials, or things that humanly speaking seem impossible, perhaps even unfair and unjust, do we say: "Why am I being given this assignment when I was doing so much good where I was?" or "Why does God allow me to encounter this 'whatever'? It is not what I want!" or "Why do I have these limitations on my health (whether at a young age or in old age)? I could be doing so much more – for the good of my Church, of souls, etc! My work is not finished!"

Of course, we forget so easily that ultimate service is not in doing – but in *being*. There are so many "whys" in our life! Humanly, it is so understandable to question, to ask "Why, Lord?" But as Priests we must strive, with the help of divine grace, to acquire Christ's attitude, to say each day, "Not my will, but yours be done" (Lk. 22:42; cf. Mt. 26:39; Mk. 14:36).

Obedience – listening to God, striving to do His will – necessarily involves the cross. In the Rite of Ordination of Priests, the ordaining Bishop says to each newly ordained Priest as he hands him the paten and chalice, "Understand what you do, imitate what you celebrate, and conform your life to the mystery of the Lord's cross." Where is the cross? The Lord reminds us that the cross will be found *daily* in the real circumstances of the "now," of everyday life. In the faithful bearing of our crosses – some small and some not so small – we learn to "have the mind of Christ" (1 Cor. 2:16; cf. Phil. 2:5) and so imitate Him in obedient self-giving and self-surrender. Of course, because of sin and our wounded human nature, we must admit that obedience is not always easy. We might, at times, have particularly heavy crosses to bear. Yet the Lord assures us, "My grace is enough for you" (2 Cor. 12:9). If a particular situation cannot be changed, can we live with it? Can we trust enough that He will resolve it in *His* time?

Pray for wisdom! To know "when" and "how" under God's light! The struggle of those in leadership is to be sure I am in tune with God through Christ's attitude of self-emptying, self-surrendering obedience to the Father's Will. Saint Paul urges us to do what Christ did: "Your attitude must be that of Christ." This is the only attitude one can have if we belong to God in Christ Jesus. Has it been? Is it? Will it be? With the example of Saint Paul and the strength of God's grace, we can say a new "yes" – *Adsum*! I come to do your will!

Poverty, chastity, obedience – if we live these three evangelical counsels in accord with our specific vocation as Priests, we can be clearer images of the love of the Heart of Jesus and more determined witnesses to His Gospel.

The challenge before us, not only during this Year for Priests but beyond, is keeping our eyes fixed on Jesus. Are we poor, chaste, and obedient? In order that we may be, each day, determined witnesses to the Gospel, let us seek the motherly intercession of Our Blessed Lady and the fraternal intercession of Saint John Mary Vianney!

I would like to close with Pope Benedict XVI's words:

> To the Most Holy Virgin I entrust this Year for Priests. I ask her to awaken in the heart of every Priest a generous and renewed commitment to the ideal of complete self-oblation to Christ and the Church which inspired the thoughts and actions of the saintly Curé of Ars. It was his fervent prayer life and his impassioned love of Christ Crucified that enabled John Mary Vianney to grow daily in his total self-oblation to God and the Church. May his example lead all Priests to offer that witness of unity with their Bishop,

with one another and with the lay faithful, which today, as ever, is so necessary. Despite all the evil present in our world, the words which Christ spoke to his Apostles in the Upper Room continue to inspire us: 'In the world you have tribulation; but take courage, I have overcome the world' (Jn 16:33). Our faith in the Divine Master gives us the strength to look to the future with confidence. Dear Priests, Christ is counting on you. In the footsteps of the Curé of Ars, let yourselves be enthralled by him. In this way you too will be, for the world in our time, heralds of hope, reconciliation and peace![28]

Yes, and I would add to these words of our Holy Father that we will be living signs of the love of the Heart of Jesus and determined witnesses to the Gospel.

---

[28] Pope Benedict XVI, *Letter Proclaiming a Year for Priests*, 16 June 2009.

Monsignor Michael Magee

Monsignor Michael Magee is a Priest of the Archdiocese of Philadelphia ordained in 1991. For the first three years of his Priesthood he was assigned to Holy Innocents Parish in Juniata Park, Philadelphia. He was then sent to Rome for studies, first at the Pontifical Biblical Institute where he obtained a Licentiate in Sacred Scripture in 1997, and then at the Pontifical Gregorian University where he obtained a Licentiate in Sacred Theology in 1998. His doctoral studies were then prolonged over the course of the next few years while fulfilling a new assignment as an Official in the Congregation for Divine Worship and the Discipline of the Sacraments, working there during the terms of Cardinals Medina and Arinze, and being occupied with many different liturgical matters, especially the examination of liturgical and biblical translations. Throughout this time, he continued writing his doctoral dissertation, which was defended and published in 2006 under the title *The Patriarchal Institution in the Church: Ecclesiological Perspectives in the Light of the Second Vatican Council*.

Upon completion of his work in Rome, he was appointed to the faculty at Saint Charles Borromeo Seminary, where he is currently Chair of the Department of Systematic Theology, Associate Professor of Systematic Theology, and Associate Professor of Sacred Scripture, serving also on the formation committees of the College and the Theology Divisions of the Seminary.

The Priesthood:
"Far more than all we ask or imagine, by the power at work within us" (Eph 3:20)

Any profession can be fulfilling when it provides someone with the opportunity to expend all of his energies and to exploit all of his talents fully in pursuit of a value that he cherishes. For me, this has certainly been true of the Priesthood. Still, it has been a continually recurring realization for me that the most rewarding moments of my Priestly ministry have been those moments when I found myself a participant in some event for which all of my combined energies and talents could not have accounted fully or even principally for the encounter with God on the part of his children that I saw being brought about through that ministry.

Certainly it was a joy whenever I could put to use all that I had learned in the many years of education that the Church had provided for me: celebrating the Rites that I had learned, honing my preaching skills, explaining the Faith in homilies or in classes, reading and speaking the languages that I had learned. But more awe-inspiring by far was what happened in those moments for which no amount of education would have been sufficient: moments that occur especially on the very boundaries of human existence, surrounded by despair and even by death, where such darkness suddenly became pervaded by a light that I could not ever have provided by my own resources or those of any other human being.

One such vignette that comes to mind occurred on an otherwise quiet day at Holy Innocents Parish in Philadelphia, when a hospice worker called to inquire about my availability to visit a man who lived only about a block or two from the rectory who was near death. I said I would certainly be able to visit that day, and I planned to stop there after completing the usual morning Communion calls. Before I had a chance to leave the rectory, however, the phone rang again. When the secretary handed me the phone, the hospice worker suggested that the man's death seemed nearer than she had previously thought, and that it might be best if I would stop by as soon as possible. Since I had been there to receive the call, I was able to be there in several minutes.

As I entered the house, I recognized the wife of the dying man, one of the many in the parish whose faces I knew without knowing their names, who were faithful Mass-goers and greeted me after Mass but never really asked for anything that would have spurred me to learn their names more quickly. I did not recognize her husband, who was placed on a bed in a central part of the house so that it would be possible for his wife and the hospice worker to be present at the same time and to move freely around the bed, and who had slipped into unconsciousness or at least semi-consciousness. Before I went in to see him, I ascertained that his wife had been very exasperated by his lapse in the practice of the Faith, but that she had convinced him before he lost full consciousness that it would be good for him to be visited by a Priest.

In several years in the Parish, only in two previous instances had it been clear to me that it would be feasible and beneficial to use the prayers prescribed by the Rites of Pastoral Care of the Sick for the moment of approaching death. This was clearly another such moment, however, since all who were present were fully aware and reconciled to the fact that the man was dying. The man could no longer speak and therefore could not make a Confession, but there was no reason to discount the possibility that he might be somewhat aware of his surroundings, so I invited him, if he could hear me, to join his heart to my words as I prayed the Act of Contrition for him, and then I gave him absolution. I then proceeded through the prayers for the dying, including this beautiful prayer:

> Go forth, Christian soul, from this world
> in the name of God the almighty Father,
> who created you,
> in the name of Jesus Christ, the Son of the living God,
> who suffered for you,
> in the name of the Holy Spirit,
> who was poured out upon you.
> Go forth, faithful Christian!
> May you live in peace this day,
> may your home be with God in Zion,
> with Mary, the Virgin Mother of God,
> with Joseph, and all the Angels and Saints. . . .

> May you return to [your Creator]
> who formed you from the dust of the earth.
> May holy Mary, the Angels, and all the Saints come to
> meet you as you go forth from this life. . . .
> May you see your Redeemer face to face.

As I was saying the words, "May you live in peace this day...", I noticed that the hospice worker, who had been looking at the man's face, looked up at his wife and nodded. When I finished the prayer, she told me that the man had died at that moment.

I recounted the story at the man's Funeral Mass, which I celebrated several days later. His wife came up to me and asked whether I could give her a copy of the prayer that I had been praying when her husband died. As it turns out, she had been terribly concerned about his soul before his death and had been hoping for some reassurance that he would not be lost despite his negligence of the practice of his Faith. The fact that his death had occurred precisely as a Priest was praying those words over him, as it turned out, was the most powerful such consolation she could possibly have received.

I would be assigned to studies in Rome very soon after that, and I was to spend the next 13 years overseas, losing contact completely with the widow, so that now I no longer even remember her name. But her story exemplifies something that had been said to me early in my stay in the same parish by the Pastor with whom I was very fortunate to be stationed in that first assignment as a Priest. After another memorable visit to a dying patient in a hospital, I had been speaking with him of the strangeness of coming away from such an awful moment yet feeling strangely uplifted. We had spoken of the privilege of being with people in that moment of passage from this life to the next, and he had observed something that I was to note myself on many other occasions. He said, "You may never see them again, but they will never forget you, because you were there for them in that moment".

Many times I experienced the truth of that observation. But the fact is that what I was able to give God's children in that moment was purely and simply the gift that had been given to me, my Priesthood. It was not my particular pastoral style, nor still less was it any words that I might be able to speak in such a moment when all human words seem so useless. More than any personal gift of mine was the consoling presence and the healing power of Christ Crucified and Risen. And very often, it was some mysterious message or sign that he gave to others through my visit or my presence, a message of which I was downright oblivious as it was being handed over to them through me.

Many times after such experiences I have likened the Priesthood to that exhilarating experience I remember when I was young, of standing just in the right place in the surf to catch the power of a large wave that lifted me up and carried me to the shore with a speed that I never could have generated by my own power. Similarly to that experience, the Priesthood requires the right equipment, and it requires putting oneself in the right place at the right time. But the exhilaration comes most of all from a power outside the self that accomplishes something that no amount of practice could ever have made possible. I have already mentioned how that power brought light even into the darkest kind of moments of the Priestly ministry, and now I will reflect upon how I have noticed the same thing happening in some of the more mundane tasks of my own Priesthood.

Homilies are certainly a Priestly activity in which preparation has a noticeable payoff: a homily carefully crafted (and interestingly, this does not always mean the longer ones!) usually elicits more grateful responses from hearers than one that is hastily done. Reading literature, watching the news, being attentive to people's hopes and fears, and especially meditating on the word of God: all of these things play a part in the work. Yet every Priest has the experience of hearing comments, whether favorable or unfavorable, on a homily that he did not realize he was preaching. The parishioner has heard the message in a way that was uniquely meaningful for him or her. The message was slightly different for each one, yet the connection with the prepared word is usually valid. The amazing thing is that when I as a Priest have found myself listening to such a reaction and thinking, "I never thought I said that", it was obviously not because the hearer was not listening, but precisely because he was listening so intently. The homilist prepares his words, and then through them, God has evidently spoken his own word. Sometimes the result is a defensive bristle at an unwelcome challenge; sometimes it is a consolation where others may have heard a criticism. But through it all, the amazing reality is that the Priest's spoken word has borne fruit in so many ways of which the Priest had no inkling even as he was preparing it or speaking it.

Perhaps for some, receiving a full-time assignment in a Seminary might be considered a detour from Priestly ministry as such, but I can honestly say I have never experienced it to be so. For me, the thrill of seeing a telling sparkle in the eyes of the students who have come to appreciate more deeply some new theological truth is more or less identical to the thrill of seeing God work through the activities that I did in a parish. In both cases, I will have been able to participate in the endeavor but not to bring about the desired result, for that depends entirely on God and on the students' cooperation with his grace. In the teaching of theology or Sacred Scripture, it is a matter not so much the transmission of an idea as it is of the unveiling of another captivating aspect of the mystery of God himself, of his love for us, or of his actions on our behalf.

The professor's preparation for a class is rewarding in itself. The exploration that must be undertaken for the sake of teaching others never ceases to yield new insights, new connections, and new points of relevance for ministry and life. Still more rewarding for me, though, is that moment when the student alights upon some new insight that had not even occurred to me in the preparation of the class. It is invigorating to share with others the fruit of my own study of some aspect of the mystery of God. But when the student, thus introduced, then continues the conversation on his own and brings something new back to the dialogue, it is a healthy reminder that unlike the other sciences to which it takes no back seat in intellectual rigor, theology has as the object of its study no mere object that can be coaxed to reveal its secrets as material nature can, but the self-revelation of the same God who declared that he can be seen by the pure of heart (Matt 5:8). The tools of the science can be imparted but the ability to engage in it depends utterly on the supernatural gift of faith. And while the Seminary professor can cooperate in many material ways, when all is said and done only God himself can form a Priest.

These few reflections on specific activities of the Priestly ministry give some concreteness, then, to my affirmation that the most rewarding aspect of the Priesthood is not so much the ability to look back on a job well done as it is the ability to see what the Lord Jesus has done even through my halting efforts, and what he continues to do after my work has ceased in regard to any given individual or community. Of course, there are many other examples that I could have given. I might mention also several occasions when persons with whom I had celebrating the Anointing of the Sick experienced recoveries immediately afterward that I could only regard as miraculous. In the three cases that come immediately to my mind, two involved patients who briefly regained consciousness long enough to put relationships in order, and then died soon after. The third was an elderly man whom I anointed with some hesitation because I thought he might already be dead, but after being anointed he quickly recovered and lived for several happy years with his wife afterward. I suspect that many more Priests than is generally known have similar experiences with this Sacrament that looks so simple but contains so much power from God.

In the three cases that I have just mentioned, it is perhaps paradigmatic of the Priestly ministry in general that while the relatives in each case attributed the otherwise inexplicably swift recovery of the person to the Anointing of the Sick, there was not a single one of those cases in which I was present to see the event. It happened immediately after I left, and if the relatives in each case had not informed me, I would not have known that it happened. This is a good thing to remember when I find myself discouraged by an apparent lack of results of ministerial work, or when I find myself with other Priests who may be likewise experience moments or periods of discouragement. And it is equally effective in counteracting a momentary burst of self-importance, which the Lord lovingly excluded for me in those instances by his timing that showed so clearly how the worker of wonders was not this flawed instrument of his, but rather the Lord himself whom I had left with his faithful disciples in the form of the Sacraments that he himself had instituted.

I imagine, then, that most of the fruits of my or anyone's Priestly ministry will remain hidden from our sight until we have been sufficiently purified in the next life to understand that those fruits were not of our own making, but to appreciate that we were nonetheless supremely privileged to be instruments in their making by the Lord himself. In fact, foremost among these is certainly the one activity that most directly defines us as Priests, namely the daily offering of the Holy Sacrifice of the Mass. Many times in doing so, I find myself troubled by the fact that the lack of time or the presence of distractions conceals from my mind, and still more from my emotions, the real impact of the awesome thing that is taking place when I hold those elements of bread and wine in my hands and speak the Savior's words over them as they are transformed into his Body and Blood. I was once intrigued to learn from another Priest who was involved with the ministries of deliverance and exorcism that there is very often a strong reaction visible in demonically possessed persons when the Holy Eucharist is carried even concealed into their presence. How odd, then, that I find myself so often challenged to appreciate with sufficient insight the significance of the Lord's presence in my own hands in such a humble form. Yet this is our lot both as human beings and as Priests: to receive God's gifts in abundance and only later to realize the greatness of what we have received.

I chuckle every time I remember one of my earliest objections to the idea of a Priestly vocation that was just beginning to plant itself in my brain when I was about twenty years old: I could not imagine what a Priest would do all day, and feared that the life of a Priest might be boring. Instead, since my Ordination nearly twenty years ago now, there have certainly been days when I would have longed for such idleness! But for the most part there have been days, months and years filled with more adventure and fulfillment than I could have thought to be possible when I was ordained. Even so, on the basis of what I have sometimes realized only after the fact, I have every reason to suspect that when by God's mercy I reach the life of heaven, my best memories of what has been accomplished through my Priesthood – including even the years from my Ordination until now – will include many things that are still hidden from my sight.

FATHER SHAWN MCKNIGHT

Rev. Shawn McKnight is a Priest of the Diocese of Wichita and the executive director of the Secretariat of Clergy, Consecrated Life, and Vocations for the United States Conference of Catholic Bishops. He earned a doctorate in sacramental theology from the Pontifical Athenaeum of Saint Anselm, Rome, and taught liturgy and homiletics at the Pontifical College Josephinum Seminary. He has served in a number of pastoral assignments, including chaplain for Newman University and pastor of Blessed Sacrament parish in Wichita, KS.

The Need for Priestly Hearts

One of the experiences I had as a newly ordained Priest years ago, taught me a lot about what it means to have a Priestly heart.

My first assignment after ordination to the Priesthood was associate pastor of Blessed Sacrament Parish in College Hill, a neighborhood in East Wichita. Shortly after my arrival, I learned of a great mystery that perplexed the pastor. After emptying the votive candle donation baskets on a weekly basis, it was becoming more evident to him that someone was lighting a number of votive candles and not making the customary donation. In fact, on one Saturday afternoon just shortly after emptying the donation baskets, the pastor walked into the church to find every votive candle lit without a single donation in any of the baskets. I remember the pastor remarking to me, "They couldn't light themselves, could they?"

While praying Daytime Prayer in the sanctuary of the church one weekday afternoon in the early spring, I heard a raucous noise entering the church. Praying while seated in a sanctuary chair near the tabernacle, and up against the east wall, I was out of view of whoever was entering the church through the east door. I heard some sort of wheels rolling on the terrazzo floor, and the clanking of metal against the door frame. Then I heard whispering, but couldn't make out what was being said. Finally, I heard the strike of the match and giggling. It was the mystery candle lighters!

Before I could close my breviary and move around the east wall of the sanctuary, I yelled out in a loud voice, "What are you doing?" Two boys were standing in front of the Our Lady of Sorrows shrine and quickly froze, matches still burning in their fingers. One of the boys was brave enough to turn toward the sanctuary and looked up at the Cross, thinking he had just heard the mighty voice of God.

When I caught sight of them, I said again, "What are you doing?" With that, the boy who rode in on his skateboard quickly departed with board under arm, through the doors, and away from the scene of the crime. The other poor fella, who had a bicycle, awkwardly maneuvered his contraption through the double doors of the church and could not make the same deft escape. As he struggled to get his bicycle through the doors with his partner in crime now gone, I moved more quickly in his direction. Frustrated and scared, he dropped his bike and made his get away.

By now my pace had quickened to a bolt, but the boys were much too fast for me. As I departed the church I could see the boy who had the bicycle running as fast as he could across the church parking lot, where at its edge the other boy was skateboarding back and forth at a distance safe from apprehension. Looking down at the bicycle at my feet, I thought to myself, "They'll be back." I then took the bike and escorted it to the garage, where I locked it up. I headed back to the church to put out all the candles they lit, and then to the school building to call the police. Justice was on the forefront of my mind.

By then the boy who dropped his bicycle recalculated his decision and decided to return to claim his property. When the young lad yelled out, "Sir," I knew he wasn't Catholic. As I turned around, the boy said, "I need my bike back."

"What were you doing in the church with your bike? And do you realize how dangerous it is to play with fire, in a church no less? Why aren't you in school?" As I said these words, I judged that I was serving my pastor well.

"We're on spring break," he responded.

Well, you can have your bicycle back but not before I call your parents. What is your name and what is your phone number?"

"No, please don't call my mom. She'll kill me," he pleaded.

"You should have thought of that before you brought your bicycle into the house of God and lit all of those candles," I said. "What is your name?"

By now, the accomplice in crime had skateboarded within earshot of all that was now transpiring.

"Brian," the boy said. "Please, give me back my bike." He gave me his home phone number, which I quickly punched into the phone just inside the door of the parish grade school. No answer. So I returned to Brian, "Are you sure you gave me the right number?"

"Yes," he said, "my mom's at work. Please, sir, don't call her at work. She doesn't need this now." At that moment, my heart began to change. I could imagine a number of things that could be going on in this boy's home life. So I said, "I tell you what, if you go into the Church with me, and kneel down and pray, then I will give you your bike back."

Brian's companion shot a big grin across his face, thinking they were getting out of this one rather easily.

We returned to the scene of the crime and stood before the statue of Our Lady of Sorrows. I said to the boys, "Do you know what this place is?"

"A church," they responded.

"And what do we do in church?" When the boys could not give the simplest answer, I knew they were unchurched. "A church is a place where people gather to pray. Sometimes they gather together, as on Sunday morning, and sometimes alone, quietly, during the middle of the day or at night. Why do you think they would come to pray by themselves?"

"They have nowhere else to go," came a response after much pondering.

"Yes, that's right. Sometimes in life, we have no place else to go. People come to pray because they need to be close to God. We Catholics also take comfort in the fact that all the Saints of heaven are not far from us, and statues like this one, remind us of their assistance. So why don't we use this church now as intended."

I struck a match and gave it to Brian and told him to light a candle. I did the same for the other boy. Then I said, "We light candles as lasting reminders of what we are praying for. Do you have something to pray for?"

"My grandmother is ill," Brian said.

I had the two boys kneel down in a pew near the shrine right away, and we prayed the Our Father together for the recovery of Brian's grandmother.

After saying the prayer, I got up and took a votive candle envelope and put a dollar in it for the two small candles we just lit. I gave it to Brian and said to him, "Here, take this offering and place it on the altar near the statute. You'll see the other envelopes there."

Brian would have none of it. "Someone could steal it!"

"Yes, that's right," I said, "but leave it there anyway. You'll be doing your part, even though someone else may take advantage of your generosity."

Brian struggled within himself to leave the envelope at the base of the statue of Our Lady of Sorrows. It was challenging for him to find justice and mercy so fused together.

As we walked out of the church, the boys apologized for their misbehavior. I unlocked the garage door and gave Brian his bicycle back. We waved good bye, and that was the last I saw of Brian and the other boy, whose name I never learned.

In the circumstances of our own times, having a Priestly heart helps to counteract all the negative publicity that is prevalent in the media about the Roman Catholic Priesthood. We have a faith that teaches us that Priests are different, that they act *in persona Christi Capitis*. But when people encounter even only a very few Priests that don't look Christ-like, we have a serious problem. One of the debilitating effects of the clergy abuse scandal is that it can test our belief in the Sacrament of Holy Orders.

Those who have accepted the charge from Christ to be shepherds (and those in formation for the Priesthood) must allow themselves to be configured by his Sacred Heart. The most effective way to counter the negative comments, attitudes, and misunderstandings about the ministerial Priesthood is for Priests to preserve the Priestly heart planted within them. And this is not always easy.

As my personal story illustrates, Priests are no different than other men when it comes to their emotions, the almost instinctive reactions that can come over us when things happen in life and ministry. But we are called to be different, to not act like the rest, to not give into temptations of selfishness, and instead to preserve the Priestly heart planted within us at ordination. The laity we encounter in our everyday ministry play a critical role in our continuing formation to be good Priests.

The people of Blessed Sacrament parish educated me in my first assignment that the Priesthood is not so much about me as it is about Jesus. My experience with the two candle lighters was great training for the young Priest that I was, and has served as a good reminder for me in my later years. It taught me about myself and what I am called to do in this life. It brought about a clearer awareness to me of why I am called to serve and whom I am called to serve. It is, unfortunately, rather easy in the business of our ministry to forget what we are fundamentally all about as Priests – to manifest the Sacred Heart in the salvation of souls.

It is my hope that Brian and the other boy would have a different take about the Roman Catholic Priesthood if and when they hear negative reports about Priests today. One never knows completely just how much of a positive impact Priests can have on other people when we learn to temper justice with mercy, when we manifest in the concrete the love that God has for all his children. The world today could certainly use more Priests, charged with the spiritual power to act *in persona Christi Capitis*, who manifest genuine Priestly hearts. Our Holy Father, Pope Benedict XVI, prays frequently for such Priests for the good of the Church and her mission, modeling personally what he has asked all Catholics to do during this "Year for Priests." May the spiritual renewal of Priests during these trying times serve to manifest the Sacred Heart of Jesus Christ throughout the world!

Rev. Joseph McLaughlin, O.Praem.

My father, John McLaughlin, died in the Naval Hospital in Philadelphia in 1950 at age 43; my brother, John, was six and I was seven. During Dad's time in the hospital, Father John McLaughlin, a Priest of the Archdiocese of Philadelphia, ministered to my father and mother. Six months before my father died, Father McLaughlin drove my brother and me to Saint Aloysius Academy in West Chester, PA, where we became boarding students for our entire elementary school years. There I made First Penance, First Communion, and Confirmation. Living among so many IHM Sisters, first in West Chester, and then in Bryn Mawr, I became aware of my desire to be a Priest. The IHM Sisters inspired me and encouraged my vocation. Upon graduation from Saint Aloysius Academy, I enrolled in Bishop Neumann High School in Philadelphia where I first met the Norbertines, especially Father Michael McLaughlin, my freshman homeroom moderator and algebra teacher. Like my father, Father Michael McLaughlin died at age 43; by then I was a Norbertine novice and one of his pall bearers. I was ordained in 1970, and, except for four years (1997-2001), have spent the rest of my Priesthood at Archmere Academy, a Norbertine high school in Claymont, Delaware. I taught English, Speech, and Religion before becoming headmaster. From 1970 to 2008 I assisted on weekends at St. Eugene Parish,

Primos, PA. During the last fifteen years I have also served concurrently as chaplain at both Villa Maria House of Studies and Saint Aloysius Academy. From Father John McLaughlin to Father Michael McLaughlin, from the IHM'S to the Norbertines, from teaching to chaplaining, God has given me "a future full of hope" (Jeremiah 29:11).

"With Eyes Undimmed and Vigor Unabated"

In the Office of Readings for June 6, Saint Norbert is described as "a most eloquent preacher: after long meditation he would preach the word of God and with his fiery eloquence purged vices refined virtues and filled souls of good will with the warmth of his wisdom" (*Christian Prayer,* Vol. 3, p. 1459). In 1978 I became Novice Master at Daylesford Abbey and in 1995 I became Chaplain at Villa Maria House of Studies; both part-time assignments brought me into deeper contact with the Scriptures (*lectio divina* with the novices, daily homilies with the sisters. Moses' words at the end of the Exodus help me reflect on my ministry as a Priest, 1970-2010: "Remember how for forty years now the Lord, your God, has directed all your journeying in the desert, so as to test you by affliction and find out whether or not it was your intention to keep His commandments. He therefore let you be afflicted with hunger, and then fed you with manna ... in order to show you that not only by bread alone does man live, but on every word that comes from the mouth of the Lord. The clothing did not fall from you in tatters, nor did your feet swell these forty years" (Deuteronomy 8:1-4; First Reading, Solemnity of Corpus Christi, Year A).

The Introduction to Deuteronomy (New American Bible) states that the events contained in the Book of Deuteronomy took place on the plains of Moab, between the end of the wanderings in the desert and the crossing of the Jordan River, a period of no more than forty days. Moses gave a series of impassioned discourses, on the eve of his death at age 120. Jesus quoted the elderly Moses three times to Satan during His temptation in the desert after His Baptism: Deuteronomy 6:13,16; 8:3; 10:20.

Although Moses was a member of the Tribe of Levi, Father John McKenzie, SJ noted that Moses was not connected with Priestly function (Dictionary of the Bible, 1965, page 588). Still, over these forty years of my Priestly ministry, Moses has been a model Priest for me and a forerunner of Jesus who through the Bishops, the successors of the apostles "continue His work as Teacher, Priest, and Shepherd" (Homily, Ordination Rite). Moses was a shepherd when called at the Burning Bush (Exodus 3:1) "to serve God's people" (Ordination Homily). About 1370 years before John the Baptist pointed out "the Lamb of God" (John 1:29), Moses directed the offering of the Passover lambs and identified the bread from heaven that the Lord provided every morning for forty years (Exodus 16:35). Also, Moses taught to the end: "Hear, O Israel! The Lord is our God, the Lord alone" (Deuteronomy 6:4). Moses was very connected to the people ("our God"). At Sinai, after the heartbreak over the golden calf, Moses said to God, "If I find favor with you, O Lord, do come along in our company. This is indeed a stiff-necked people; yet pardon our wickedness and sins, and receive us as your own" (Exodus 34:9). Moses remained among the people (Hebrews 5:1).

At the time of his call at the Burning Bush, Moses said to God, "If you please, Lord, I have never been eloquent, neither in the past, nor recently, nor now that you have spoken to your servant; but, I am slow of speech and tongue" (Exodus 4:10). But there was amazing eloquence forty years later, in the plains of Moab, as Moses prepared to die outside the Promised Land, with the Promise of God alive in his heart: "I will take you as my own people, and you shall have me as your God" (Exodus 6:7). Such heartfelt confidence, born of face-to-face encounters (Deuteronomy 34:10), enabled Moses to be a very persuasive preacher during all the forty years, as the following texts indicate:

1. "Go and procure lambs for your families, and slaughter them as Passover victims" (Exodus 12:21);
2. "Remember this day on which you came out of Egypt" (Exodus 13:3);
3. "Fear not! Stand your ground, and you will see the victory the Lord will win for you today" (Exodus 14:13);
4. "This is the bread which the Lord has given you to eat" (Exodus 16:15);
5. "You have committed a grave sin. I will go up to the Lord, then; perhaps I may be able to make atonement for your sins" (Exodus 32:30);
6. "Why are you again disobeying the Lord's orders? This cannot succeed" (Numbers 14:41);

7. "Listen to me you rebels! Are we to bring water for you out of this rock" (Numbers 20:10);
8. "The Lord, your God, has given this land over to you. Go up and occupy it, as the Lord, the God of your fathers, commands you. Do not fear or lose heart" (Deuteronomy 1:21);
9. "Now, Israel, hear the statutes and decrees which I am teaching you to observe, that you may live, and may enter in and take possession of the land which the Lord, the God of your Fathers, is giving you" (Deuteronomy 4:1).
10. "How fortunate you are, O Israel! Where else is a nation victorious in the Lord? The Lord is your saving shield" (Deuteronomy 33:29).

Moses' final words in the Book of Deuteronomy are words of blessing. Just as the Israelites had arrived at the end of their forty-year journey with untattered clothes and unswollen feet, so Moses blessed (spoke well) to the end; "his eyes were undimmed and his vigor unabated" (Deuteronomy 34:7).

In August of 1978 I made a private retreat at Saint Joseph's Abbey in Spencer, Massachusetts. On the last day of retreat I spoke to the novice master, Father Joseph, OCSO, asking advice as I began my new duties as novice master at Daylesford Abbey. He told me to use Sacred Scripture as the basis for all my formation work. Within two weeks I began the daily practice of *lectio divina* with the novices, beginning with the Gospel of

Mark. The daily hour of lectio has helped me to "hear the word of God and act on it" (Luke 8:21).

Shortly before she died on February 8, 1985, Sister Marie Antoine, IHM, former president of Immaculata College, asked me to preach at her funeral; she gave me one directive: "Speak only on the Scriptures." That advice has guided me through my daily homilies at the IHM Motherhouse these last fifteen years.

My homilies have evolved over these forty years, from references to the novels and short stories I was teaching, to stories from newspapers and *Sports Illustrated*, to the sequential events of each day's Gospel, and, during the Easter Season, from the Acts of the Apostles. As Saint Paul wrote, "Let the word of Christ, rich as it is, dwell in you" (Colossians 3:16). *Lectio divina* helps that Word each day to bear fruit in my heart. As the Bishop says during the Ordination Homily, "Share with all mankind the Word of God you have received with joy. Meditate on the law of God, believe what you read, teach what you believe, and put into practice what you teach." *Lectio divina* has helped me move from the halting speech at the Burning Bush to the grateful praise on the Plains of Moab.

The author of The Epistle to the Hebrews wrote, "Moses was faithful in all God's household as a servant charged with the task of witnessing to what could be spoken; but Christ was faithful as the Son placed over God's house" Hebrews 3:5-6). As I mark my fortieth anniversary as a Priest, I remember how for forty years now God has directed all my journeying, feeding me with every word that comes from the mouth of the Lord (cf. Deuteronomy 8:1-4), to be a servant charged with witnessing to what could be spoken. I am relying on God's word anew as I begin my new assignment as chaplain at Archmere Academy.

In the IHM Sisters' "Canticle of Praise" (1995), "The God of Boundless Love, ever-saving Lord (calls) us to Mary's heart, temple of the Word, to lives of selfless giving, to love's redeeming way." As I continue to travel "love's redeeming way" with Moses of Egypt and Jesus of Nazareth, I say, "For all that has been, for all that will be, Praise, Love, Thanksgiving, our God, to Thee" (IHM *Canticle of Praise*).

MONSIGNOR FRANCIS X. MEEHAN

Monsignor Meehan received his Doctorate in Moral Theology in 1965 at the Academia Alfonsiana, (Lateran University.) He also spent the year 1973-74 in a program of Spirituality at Saint Louis University. Over the years he has taught at Bishop Shanahan High School, Cardinal Dougherty, Saint Charles Borromeo Seminary Theologate, and also the Religious Studies Division. He has taught at Immaculata College, at LaSalle University, including a summer at The Catholic University of America. He wrote, in 1982, a book, titled "A Contemporary Spirituality."

Over the years he has written several pamphlets and many articles for an array of Catholic publications including his writing for the Archdiocesan paper, *The Catholic Standard and Times*, – 25 years as a monthly columnist. He has lectured widely including giving retreats and other talks to Priests, religious and lay groups. He was a consultant on one occasion for the Vatican Office of Justice and Peace as well as participating in various programs for the National Conference of Catholics Bishops.

For the past 20 years he has been in parish work, 18 of which have been as pastor of Saints Simon and Jude Parish in West Chester. Retired in June, 2007, the Cardinal assigned him to the role of an adjunct spiritual director at Saint Charles Borromeo Seminary.

Integrating the Liturgy of the Hours into Personal Prayer

Introduction

I have set out to write here in a manner more befitting a senior Priest looking back and saying a large "thank you, dear loving God, for an insight along the way." The following thoughts are less theological, more pastoral. Yet the two modes of thought should never be placed in opposition to one another.

The main purpose of my words below is to reflect on how the Liturgy of the Hours can be transformed. The Office (literally the *officium*, the "duty") can become, with God's grace, less a duty and more a healing personal grace from the Heart of Christ.

Saint John Vianney's words on the meaning of Priesthood are recalled: "Priesthood is the Love of the Heart of Jesus!" The Heart of Christ can act upon us within even dutiful prayers. The Psalms can have a healing impact on our spirits, on our day of ministry.

The Liturgy of the Hours was designed first to be sung in choir and community. The transferal to the private life of a Priest, religious, or layperson has never been an easy one. (Everything I say here can be applied by the many lay people and Religious into their own ways of life and ministry in the Church. In fact, it was our Men's Scripture Group's praying of Lauds every Saturday morning for some 16 years that gave me insights into how the Heart of Christ could nurture within them a vibrant lay spirituality.)

How can this love of the Heart of Christ be integrated into an ordinary day of ministry? Devotion to the Heart of Christ could seem distant from the daily "recitation" of the Breviary, yet there can be ways to overcome the distance. But, first, let me speak a simple autobiographical note regarding the Heart of Christ as a familiar devotion!

The Gift of an Early Image

Devotion to the Heart of Christ came to me in very early years. In the late 1940s, my brother, Father Jim Meehan, 11 years my senior, while he was in the Seminary, brought to our family a prominent devotion of the time, titled "The Enthronement of the Sacred Heart in the Home." Our parents – filled with faith – led us in the way of this devotion.

In those early years of grade school and then in high school, we would, – each of us in the family – take an hour of prayer on a First Friday or First Thursday evening. We would do this in the living room before a wonderful image of the Sacred Heart. (The painting can now be found in the Reconciliation Room of Saints Simon and Jude Church in West Chester, PA.)

We used a booklet of prayers in those days. The booklet still – when I pick it up – reads fresh. I do not think I ever totally allowed the gift of this devotion to fall from my horizon, even though there surely have been dry times. I mention this to signal what follows, namely our effort to see this moment of devotional life applied to the praying of the Liturgy of the Hours.

The Struggle for Integration

It has been said that "Saint John Mary Vianney did not content himself with the ritual carrying out of the activities of his ministry. It was his heart and his life which he sought to conform to Christ. It is this one thought that underlies this article: namely to move from ritual to heart, from duty to healing devotion in our praying of the Office.

Early on in my Priesthood, moral theologian and Redemptorist Father, Bernard Haring once told us: "Be careful in praying the Office – not to allow it to become a teacher of how *not* to pray." He was basically warning against a kind of legalism, a scrupulosity of the times, a "merely-getting-in-the-duty," the loss of a certain freedom of spirit, the absence of any real lifting of heart."

More and more, in my life as a Priest – perhaps a matter of age, I suppose – one begins to appreciate the Liturgy-of-the-Hours' potential for a real transformation of personal prayer. Not that praying the Hours is easy, not that there are not times of rust and dryness, and wonderings and confusion, not that there are not times when the words are as chalk in our mouths, – yet, there is within the Hours a rooting, a grounding, a healing, a truly devotional blessing.

We are rooted in prayer, in the Lord, in the Church, in the community. We are grounded in the Psalms Jesus spoke to His Father. His power speaks within us. This ancient way of the-Church-at-prayer can become the "love of the Heart of Christ" healing our day and our ministry.

Allow me to touch on three simple examples: In a way, my choices are arbitrary. Each one could choose his or her favorite Psalms and prayers, and the special way the Heart of Christ can be found in them: The three I have chosen are these: 1) Morning Prayer: The Heart of Christ giving us courage for our upcoming day's ministry, 2) Evening Prayer: The wisdom of the Heart of Christ entering into our ministry, 3) Night Prayer (Compline): A gift of affectivity from the Heart of Christ for those who have given up home and family.

Morning Prayer: A Time to Cast Our Fears on the Lord

Let us begin with Lauds, Monday morning of the First Week, Ordinary Time: The Psalm Prayer of that Monday morning reminds me of one simple thing that can inhibit the life of many Priests, including my own, – namely our fears. *"May your face shine upon us, O Lord, and keep us in peace."*

A parish Priest can have so many fears. I was encouraged by once having read Father Henri Nouwen's account of his fears. He saw fear as something deeper and more pervasive that we often suspect. The fears and anxieties of ministry can be very subtle: Who is going to be angry with me this day; what conflict will arise this week; what decision must I make today; is there a difficult person I may have to deal with? The Heart of Christ, can heal fears, give courage, grant suppleness to our speech, even a wise flexibility to our administration.

There is within Lauds a kind of preparation to go out to be among God's people. A Psalm Prayer prays:

> Lord send your mercy and your truth to rescue us from the snares of the devil, and, happy to be known as companions of your Son, we will praise You among the peoples and proclaim you to the nations.

We start our day, with a sudden and deep realization of what a day of ministry can be – a praising of God among the peoples.

Amazing how a Psalm or a Psalm-Prayer can be a moment for knowing God is with us. Saint Paul tells us: *"The Spirit which God has given us is not a cowardly spirit, but one that makes us strong loving and wise."* And Peter tells us to *"cast your cares upon the Lord."*

I have also noticed how the Saturday (Week I) Psalms and the Psalm Prayer hold such power: Saturday morning can be the beginning of a busy day of weddings, funerals, vigil Masses, appointments. The prayer reminds us of the Heart of Christ's mercy pervading our spirit, and working through us: *"Save us by the power of your hand, Father...May the fire of your word consume our sins."* *"May Jesus who is called faithful and true, possess our hearts forever."* The Heart of Christ can possess our hearts through the day, even when we are not explicitly in prayer!

In Morning Prayer, we can thus take a moment in the Psalm or between a Psalm, just to allow the Lord's courage to seep through, as we imagine the upcoming events of our day. Sometimes with pad and pencil in hand, we can glance forward to our day or our week, and jot down tasks that may carry with them a certain anxiety. Even the human aspect of this is helpful; it allows me to name little burdens hidden in our unconscious, and secretly upsetting us. This is not just good psychology. It is also a spirituality! In the Liturgy of the Hours, the Church has given us a daily regimen for *"casting our cares upon the Lord." "Come to me, you who labor and are burdened. Take my yoke upon you."* Too often we work with our own yoke made heavy by our fears, rather than the lighter yoke of the Lord.

The day moves on. Lauds has become not just a duty, but truly a prayer! A gift occurs: Now we do not say, "Thank God, I've gotten Lauds over; now I can maybe find time for a personal prayer." Lauds, prayed with a certain freedom of spirit, – a hesitation here, a quiet space there – is suddenly integrated into our personal prayer. The Liturgy of the Hours may have been first arranged for public, communitarian prayer. Yet now it can become a personal devotion as well. There is an intercession in Morning Prayer that says, *"Through your risen Son, you sent the Holy Spirit into*

the world, set our hearts on fire with spiritual love."
Heart of Christ, speak to our hearts through these everyday Psalms, readings, and petitions!

Evening Prayer: The Wisdom of the Heart of Christ

Now, let us take an ordinary Tuesday evening in the Parish. Tuesday is a meeting night, if there ever was one: Pastoral Council, Finance Council, CYO, Home and School, CCD.

During my years in parish ministry, I was, after dinner, often too fixed on trying to watch a little news before attending meetings. Later, I began to realize the gift of a calm praying of Vespers. A Psalm Prayer of Vespers leaps off the page: *"Almighty God, remember our lowliness, and have mercy..."* Often, after finishing the Psalms, I might stop and try a few minutes of Centering Prayer. This combination of Vespers and Centering seemed to have a good effect on my composure. The Heart of Christ seems to have a way of gathering all of our distractions in, and can even give us greater wisdom in all that we have to do that evening at the various meetings. Of course, I was not always wise, but the prayer of Vespers began to help animate within me a more confident and composed presence.

Often, through the years, I had had the practice of taking telephone calls right before meetings – as a way of "getting this call out of the way" rather than having to return calls the next day. The praying of Vespers, instead of watching television and taking calls, began to relieve a certain compulsivity to get everything too "done"! I know, in my case, that the tendency to want to get things done too quickly would often end in *un-wisdom,* or a manner that was much too "all business."

I do not mean to say I was always successful in these more prayerful ways of approaching an evening's work. I wish I had been more consistent through the years.

I have often cherished what Saint Gregory spoke about in the great reading contained in the Breviary. Gregory's words took me by surprise in their freshness and applicability to our lives; they apply not only to those in parish ministry, but to teachers, parents, religious – everyone! Here is an excerpt from his famous reflection:

> Anyone appointed to be a watchman for the people must stand on a height for all his life to help them by his foresight... I do not deny my responsibility; I recognize that I am slothful and negligent... Since I assumed the burden of pastoral care, my mind can no longer be collected; it is concerned with so many matters. I am forced to consider the affairs of the Church...With my mind divided and torn to pieces by so many problems, how can I meditate or preach wholeheartedly.... So who am I to be a watchman, for I do not stand on the mountain of action but lie down in the valley of weakness? Truly the All powerful Creator and Redeemer of humankind can give me in spite of my weaknesses a higher life and effective speech; Because I love him, I do not spare myself in speaking of him.

Vespers, freely said, spoken in peace, – some of it given over to quiet – can be a prayer to counter this "Gregory tendency" within us. A Psalm Prayer from Tuesday (Week II) sums up everything: *"Make our mouths speak your wisdom, Lord Jesus..."* The Heart of Christ, through a simple pause within Vespers, can say to us: *"Come to me, you who labor and are burdened... Tonight I will be with you."*

A Priest's "Day Off": A Compline Prayer for Those Who Have Given Up Home and Family.

Days off are not always easy for Priests. Some are blessed with family connections, but all are challenged to find a rhythm of leisure, of friends – a rhythm that includes the blessing of Priest-friends as well. For a day off, each of us have different situations, different personalities. Some have the gift of initiative. Some are good self-starters, and can find something creative to do. Some find a moment of aloneness helpful. Others struggle with too much aloneness.

Psalm 143 (Tuesday Compline) can say so much to us about judiciousness, and creativity in our scheduling of work and leisure. *"Lord .... to you I stretch out my hands. Like a parched land my soul thirsts for you. Lord, make haste and answer me; for my spirit fails within me. Do not hide your face...Make me know the way I should walk; teach me to do your will. Let your good spirit guide me in ways that are level and smooth."*

The life of a celibate means a certain homelessness. Yet, small places of refuge can be helpful. I once read a helpful phrase from writer/scholar and Holy Cross Father, John Dunne. He urged celibates to become aware of what he called *"the little givings and receivings"* of our lives. He means by this phrase for us to accept graciously and to truly internalize such things as small compliments given to us, or affirmations, and, yes, the giving receiving of simple meetings with friends and family. In these little "givings and *receivings*," our spirit can be liberated – by God's grace – from grasping for too large a giving and receiving.

Compline or Night Prayer can be a moment for internalizing the "little givings and *receivings*" of our day. At the end of a week, in need of a regular rhythm of leisure, we can turn into "a parched land." Yet the Heart of Christ within a Psalm can heal our affectivities, our psyche, our many inner needs and weaknesses.

One could stop on any night for just a few moments and make the great commendation of Compline a mantra for a few minutes of very restful prayer. *"Into your hands, Lord, I commend my spirit; you have redeemed us, Lord God of truth. Into your hands I commend my spirit."*

Concluding Reflection:
A Realistic Recognition of the Difficulty of Integration
There is so much one could say about transforming our "Office" into a personal prayer of devotion. I know of no

one who has not found the Liturgy of the Hours a challenging mode of prayer – at least at times. Sometimes there just seems to be too many words! Too many thoughts! We cannot do violence to the mind by trying to invest everything with powerful meaning. In fact, for some of us, instead, we may have to look up, skip a paragraph or so, stay quiet in God's freedom, know the Heart of Christ is with us in our weakness.

None of what is said above should be taken to counter the efforts of Priests, lay and religious to include in our day longer moments of contemplative prayer, whether it be Ignatian Prayer, Centering Prayer, or *Lectio Divina*. Yet it is good to recognize that we might, through the grace of God, find a way of integrating a little bit of each of these methods into our praying of the Breviary.

I end where I began: When we were young, our family was blessed to sit for an hour before a great image of the Sacred Heart. That was known, and is still known as a "devotion." The Liturgy of the Hours is known as... well... the Liturgy of the Hours. But it is truly also a devotion, a love. Personal prayer, liturgical prayer, public prayer, prayer of the church, devotion, healing, mercy – none of these can be set off from one another.

Teach us how to pray, O Holy Spirit. When we do not know how to pray, Saint Paul consoles us by letting us know that the Holy Spirit prays within us with unutterable groanings. As was said above, "Saint John Mary Vianney did not content himself with the ritual carrying out of the activities of his ministry. It was his heart and his life which he sought to conform to Christ." The Heart of Christ can speak to our hearts through the Psalms, prayers and simple readings of a daily "Office." May the Holy Spirit teach each one of us to find the way of John Vianney that integrates the ritual and duty of the Liturgy of the Hours with love and devotion.

Rev. Donald Miniscalco, C.Ss.R.

Father Donald Miniscalco, a Philadelphia native, is currently stationed at St. Peter's Church, 5th and Girard Avenue, the Shrine of Saint John Neumann. Father is a Redemptorist Priest, ordained in 1968. He pursued doctoral studies at the Sorbonne University in Paris and the Gregorian University in Rome and has taught in various seminaries and universities in this country. Father also has served at parishes in Buffalo and New York City's colorful Lower East Side.

Since 1980, Father Don has devoted full time and energy to conducting parish Missions. Although he works primarily in the Philadelphia region, he has also conducted renewals in Ireland, Canada and the Caribbean and has directed retreats for Priests, religious sisters and lay people in the United States and abroad.

In 2003, Pope John Paul II bestowed the *Pro Ecclesia et Pontifice* honor on Father Miniscalco at the request of the Archdiocese of Philadelphia in recognition of his service in the new evangelism.

The Priest as Missionary

As a young Priest studying in Paris forty years ago, I often slipped into the Jesuit church on the *rue de Sevres*. Sometimes, I just needed a place where my brain could stop spinning after an erudite Gallic lecture. As one entered Saint Ignace, a placard – and I hope it's still there – struck the eye: a picture of Saint Francis Xavier and a quotation of a letter he wrote from India in 1544:

> Many times I am seized with the thought of crying out like a mad man, telling those in the Sorbonne who have greater regard for learning than desire to prepare themselves to produce fruit with it: Thousands upon thousands, and millions upon millions are waiting to hear God's Word. And I felt that not one student is willing to say 'Here I am, Lord. What do you want me to do?' like Samuel in the Bible. "Send me wherever you will, and if need be, even to the Indies.

Send me. I've been asked to write about 'sending,' mission, as a component of Priestly spirituality. Evidently, we are not writing a complete treatise. Very little will be said on topics about which very much should be said, for example, the apostolic spirituality the Apostle Paul gives us, the 'new evangelization,' the use of modern communications media like the Internet, the Priest as missionary catalyst in a parish. Instead, we focus on a few, very basic missionary elements in Priestly spirituality.

Since he acts *in persona Christi,* any authentic spirituality for a Priest originates in and is sustained by his identification, his configuration to, his love of the Lord Jesus. Otherwise, the Priest is reduced to an employee of an ecclesiastical organization desperately trying to maintain itself. Such a Priest either drudges on as a functionary or plays a game career advancement.

The Gospels show us Jesus, to whom ordination configures the Priest, purposely defining the activity he embarks upon as a mission. Deliberately, at his inaugural sermon at Nazareth, he unrolls the scroll a passage which emphasizes being sent by the Lord to proclaim glad tidings and a time of grace: The spirit of the Lord is upon me, therefore he has anointed me. He has sent me to bring glad tidings to the poor, to proclaim liberty to captives, recovery of sight to the blind, release to prisoners, and to announce a year of favor from the Lord. (Lk 4:17-19; cf Is 61:1ff). Even if 'sight to the blind' refers to physical healing, we see already the primary purpose of Jesus' being sent is to bring good news (to evangelize – *euangelizesthai*), to proclaim (to act as a herald – *keryxai*). The basic nexus – mission-evangelization – is established.

While Jesus in the Synoptics defines what he does as a mission, we find something even more profound in the Gospel of John. There, Jesus continually defines and identifies his own Self as the One whom the Father sends and invokes the Father as the One who has sent him (e.g. Jn 4:34; 5:30, 36, 37).

If we had to encapsulate the good news in one verse, would it not be Jn 3:16, which cameras at football games now avoid – *God so loved the world that he gave his only son*? The very next verse of the passage links the concept 'giving' with 'sending.' God did not send his Son into the world to condemn the world. The Father sends Jesus as his Gift. Because of his configuration with Jesus, the One-sent, the Priest realizes profoundly: he too is a gift of the Father to those to whom he has been sent.

Furthermore, the Fourth Gospel often presents the act of faith as acceptance of Jesus precisely as the One sent by the Father. Even his compassionate and merciful response to human needs, his 'signs,' in the Fourth Gospel terminology, are done to provide the motive for believing his claim to be sent by the Father. Perhaps an oversimplification, but one might say that in the Synoptics, Jesus is sent to proclaim. In John, he is sent because he is the Word. In this regard, anyone who hears the Gospel, might reflect on John 9. We are all born blind and ordered by Christ to plunge into the waters of Siloam, 'the One who has been sent. *A fortiori*, Christ commands the Priest to plunge into his mystery as the One who is sent.

Jesus, conscious not only of his own mission, consciously exercises his authority to choose and send others to evangelize, to announce the kingdom and do works which authenticate and actualize their proclamation. Although he will send seventy-two disciples, we notice the special selection of the Twelve who will be with him, (Mk 3:14), a prerequisite for his sending them (Mk 6:7).

Scripture provides many images of those whom Christ chooses for that special closeness to him. As just one example, they are stewards, dispensing the grain in due season, awaiting their master's return, with authority to care for, not abuse, the others in the household. Perhaps every Priest cherishes most dearly the shepherd image. I've had the joy of leading over fifty Priests' retreats. On Friday morning, Priests are ready to run after concelebrating Mass. Even as they pack suitcases and strip beds, though, the Good Shepherd theme holds their attention and leads to very heart-felt prayer, particularly if Jn 21:15-17 is the text for the morning conference. Jesus to Peter – Do you love me? Peter – You know that I love. And Jesus' mandate – Feed my sheep,

However, another image also evokes a mandate of Christ to those whom he chooses: fishers of men. Jesus chooses actual fishermen as his companions. He molds them and sends them as fishers of men (Mk 1:17. Mt 4:19). Significantly, the Gospel of Luke, emphasizes this missionary dimension of the whole Church and specifically of the apostles at the very beginning. Jesus commands them to leave the safety of the shoreline and to put out into the deep. After the miraculous catch of fish, he tells Simon and the others not to be afraid or even be dismayed by their own sinfulness because he intends that from now on they will be catching men. Christ's Church and his apostles are meant for more than hugging the shoreline. They are sent into the deep.

The image of fishermen sent out into the deep, willing at Jesus' word, to lower the nets though it seem futile, conveys a much more unsettled activity than shepherd imagery. Although the shepherd does indeed speak to his sheep, his voice primarily guides along the right paths. The fisherman's voice, on the other hand, heralds good news and summons to conversion. He evangelizes, which Cardinal Avery Dulles very succinctly defines: In the New Testament, evangelize means to proclaim with authority and power the good news of salvation offered in Jesus Christ (Dulles. *Evangelization for the Third Millennium*. Paulist Press, 2009, 1). The apostle is sent primarily to proclaim the good news. "Proclamation is the permanent priority of mission. The church cannot elude Christ's explicit mandate nor deprive men and women of the good news about their being loved and saved by God" (*Redemptoris Missio*, 44). Saint Paul designates himself and others who proclaim the Gospel as apostles (e.g. for himself Rm 1:1 I Cor 1:1 etc.; for others who are not the Twelve Rm 16:7; 1 Cor 12:28; Eph 4:11 etc). He uses 'ambassador' (e.g.2 Cor 5:20) in the same way. When 'sent' is used, it is almost always linked to the explicit proclamation of the gospel.

It would be both futile and foolish to oppose biblically rich images, for example the shepherd to the fisher since all express authentic aspects of Priestly spirituality. The danger comes if we neglect the missionary – apostolic dimension of Priesthood. Technically, because of their full configuration to Christ, the responsibility to proclaim the Gospel falls primarily to Bishops (*Ad Gentes* 29, also *Lumen Gentium*, 25). What though of the Priest who collaborates in the apostolic ministry?

The vast majority of Priests, of course, engage in parish life where quite rightly the role of shepherd predominates but might risk obliterating the missionary-apostolic aspect of the Priestly vocation. Did Paulist Father Robert Rivers, a Priest with much expertise in parish ministry, express the problem too starkly when he titled his book on evangelization in the parish *From Maintenance to Mission*? We might validly ask: is the Priest meant only as a maintainer without being a missionary? How many parish "mission statements" even acknowledge Christ's mandate to evangelize? Almost all that I've read look inward. Very few look at fields white with harvest.

In a 2005 lecture, Cardinal Dulles traced what he calls the crisis of evangelization to the Counter-Reformation. "Missionary activity still went on, but it was seen as the preserve of apostolic religious orders and societies rather than the concern of the Church as a whole" (Dulles, *op cit* p 2). Dulles contends that Pope Paul VI's *Evangelii Nuntiandi* halted misinterpreting Vatican II as concerned only with internal issues. Still, the partial eclipse of the Church's missionary dimension has contributed to a lessening of the missionary character of the Priestly vocation.

In recent years, two trends in the Church worldwide, evident also in the United States, have devalued the missionary aspect of Priestly life. A saying attributed to Saint Francis of Assisi: *"Preach the Gospel at all times; use words if necessary"* is the first trend's slogan. No scholar can find such words in any writing of or about Saint Francis. Francis did say in the Rule of 1221, "let all the friars preach by their deeds." Who doubts that Christians must witness the Gospel by their actions or that such witness is a primary method of announcing it, evidently what Il Poverello meant? In *Evangelii Nuntiandi*, Paul VI makes the point even more trenchantly that "modern man listens more willingly to witnesses than to teachers, and if he does listen to teachers, it is because they are witnesses." (cf also John Paul II *Redemptoris Missio*, 42) However, the Pope goes on: "even the finest witness will prove ineffective if it is not explained, justified and made explicit by a clear and unequivocal proclamation of the Lord Jesus" (*Evangelii Nuntiandi* 22).

Far more seriously, the revival of an ancient idea known as *apocatastasis* that all rational creatures will eventually be saved challenges the Church's teaching that all people have at least the *possibility* of salvation even if they have not explicitly heard the gospel. In practice if (almost) everyone will be saved anyway, why should anyone be sent to announce an offer of salvation? Is the Church as a whole and the Priest as apostle sent on a fool's errand? In his combat with the Jansenist view that God offers only 'limited atonement,' and that Christ died for only the predestined, Saint Alphonsus Liguori insisted on the Scripture text I Timothy 2:4: *God wills all men to be saved and come to the knowledge of the truth* and chose as the motto for his Redemptorists – *Copiosa apud eum redemptio* – "With him there is plentiful redemption" (Psalm 130). Naturally, as a Redemptorist, I rejoice in the specific charism of proclaiming the plenteous redemption. However, a Religious only lives in a specific manner a charism belonging to the Church as a whole and, as we have seen in our consideration of the missionary-apostolic dimension, to the Priesthood as a whole. How are all to *come to the knowledge of the truth* that God wills their salvation without being told? And who above all must do the telling if not the Priest, configured to Jesus, the One sent.? The motto of Saint Charles Borromeo Seminary in Philadelphia is worth reflection. *Exiit qui seminat* – "The sower went out" (Mt 13:3). The Priest-sower who goes forth. He doesn't just wander out. He is sent to sow the Word of God.

The embrace of this missionary aspect enriches Priestly spirituality. Conversely, its absence can impoverish it. Fortunately in these days of parish business managers and plant supervisors, less of a Priest's time and energy goes into the five "L's" – lights, locks, litter, leaks, and loot – the bane of a Priest's life *in diebus illis*. Supposedly, he is freer to do Priestly ministering. However, if the Priest concentrates solely or almost exclusively on ministering to the multiple needs and demands of his flock, he risks seriously fragmenting his identity as a Priest. In a delicate change of nuance, a more mission oriented spirituality shifts from 'to what need must I minister' to 'what have I, as a Priest, been sent here to do?' Others may indeed be gifted to minister to this or that need. But what have I as a Priest been sent to do? The Priest, to whom Jesus is Master, Teacher, Savior, Healer, Lord, relates to him also as Sender, the person who sends him personally into the world.

The Church locates the establishment of the Priesthood at the Last Supper. The sending forth of the apostles on mission to proclaim the Kingdom is not their ordination. However, it may aid in appreciating the depth of Priestly mission spirituality to reflect on Jesus' prayer in John, which does not record the institution of the Eucharist and concomitant institution of the Priesthood. This prayer manifests the profound bond between Christ who is the consecrating Priest and consecrated sacrificial victim and the Priest who is united with him as one sent into the world to proclaim the truth, Christ himself.

> Consecrate them by means of truth –
> 'Your word is truth.'
> As you have sent me into the world,
> So also I have sent them into the world;

> I consecrate myself for their sake now,
> that they may be consecrated in truth.

Awesome, our teenagers would say. Pope Benedict would say *audacious*. Here, we need not examine the aorist [I *have* sent] or how 'disciples' – John's term for Jesus' chosen – are now the ones Jesus sends, [*apesteila autous*]. Jesus is offering himself in sacrifice for the ones he is sending into the world so that they may be totally set aside for God, consecrated, and sent into the world with his word which is true. What a totally humbling yet exalted understanding of the Priesthood.

Second, the Scripture stresses the many virtues of shepherding. In I Peter, for example, the presbyters, must care for the flock, guard it willingly, not for profit, not lording it over them, etc. No doubt, good shepherding requires the cultivation of the Spirit's fruits such as patience and humility, even meekness, traits foreign to our culture. Scripture also indicates virtues associated with the sense of mission, these, too, counter-cultural, perhaps the most alien being the ascesis of traveling light. Jesus' directs those he sends on mission to take what they actually need, not haul baggage which only slows them down and not be deflected from their mission of evangelizing through entanglement with extraneous matters, what we call staying focused. Although without research to validate my anecdotal observations in the various dioceses where I have been asked to help Priests involved in sexual abuse, I would say that almost always they have lived rather cushy lives indistinguishable from rampant American consumerism. Those who never denied themselves material comfort could not restrain sexual indulgence. I wonder what the study of the causes of the abuse commissioned by the Bishops will show.

Finally, we see a particular tone of manliness which greatly enhances the spiritual life of any Priest considered as one sent. Again not a matter of missionary spirituality being opposed to pastoral spirituality because the good shepherd sees the wolf coming and defends his sheep. The shepherd has courage, does not run away in the face of danger. The missionary, though, plays more offense than defense. The Acts of the Apostles ends with the word *parrhesia,* generally translated 'assurance' or 'boldness' a characteristic of proclaiming the Gospel. Its opposite is *deilia ,*'cowardice.' Specifically referring to ordination, the Apostle Paul writes in 2 Timothy: "I remind you to stir into flame the gift of God that you have received through the imposition of my hands. For God did not give us a spirit of cowardice but one of power and love and self-control."

While Scripture certainly does not approve nor anyone want a rude, boorish or bellicose Priest, a confused age cries out for the boldness in proclaiming the Gospel given in ordination. If nothing else, the Priest will gain grudging respect because he did not shrink from what the world expects him to be doing. "But how shall they call on him in whom they have not believed? And how can they believe unless they have heard of him? And how can they hear unless there is someone to preach? And how can men preach unless they are sent?" For Scripture says, "How beautiful are the feet of those who announce the good news" (Rm 10:14-15).

This fall, Pope Benedict will beatify John Henry Newman, prodigious scholar, masterful preacher, astute spiritual guide. In 1849, Newman addressed "The Prospects of a Catholic Missioner." at the inauguration of the London Oratory. He spoke of a vast population only an aggregate of solitary individuals, where 'no one knows his next-door neighbor and each one is pursuing his own interests," and of a culture which "like the ocean closes over every attempt made to influence and impress it." Could he also be describing bewildered, Facebook America? Yet, he says, at the most inauspicious time, Peter a Galillean fisherman, entered Rome. Such has been the case throughout the centuries in the examples he cites. Then Newman concludes:

> It is no new thing then with the Church in a time of confusion or of anxiety when the enemy is at her gates, that her children, far from being dismayed but rather glorying in the danger as vigorous men exult in trials of their strength, go forth to do her work as though she were in the most palmy days of her prosperity. *We Catholics do not know when we are beaten; we advance when by all the*

rules of war we ought to fall back. [30]

We advance because we know the One who sends us, who consecrates us his Priests, the one who has the audacity to send not only Francis Xavier to India but even us to twenty-first century America.

---

[30] Daniel M. O'Connell. Favorite Newman Sermons. America Press, 1940. Page 210.

Rev. Brian Mulcahy, O.P.

Father Brian Martin Mulcahy, O.P. was born in 1962 in Harare, Zimbabwe to parents who were career diplomats in the U.S. Foreign Service. Father Brian graduated from Notre Dame International School in Rome, Italy, and from the University of Virginia with a BA (Honors) in English. He entered the Order of Preachers upon graduating from the University and made his first profession of vows on August 15, 1985. He pursued his studies for the Priesthood at the Pontifical Faculty of the Immaculate Conception (Dominican House of Studies) in Washington, DC, and was ordained a Priest May 24, 1990 at Saint Dominic's Church, Washington, by Bishop Louis Gelineau of the Diocese of Providence, RI. Since ordination, his assignments have included a brief time as parochial vicar of Saint Mary's Church, New Haven, CT; 2 1/2 years as a staff member in the doctrinal section of the Congregation for the Doctrine of the Faith in Rome; hospital ministry in New York City; 7 months as chaplain to the Monastery of Dominican Nuns in Buffalo, NY; and subprior and parochial vicar at Saint Dominic's Church, Youngstown, OH from 1997-2002. While in Youngstown, Father Brian also served from 1998-2002 as Director of the Newman Center at Youngstown State University. In 2002, he became pastor and superior at Saint Thomas Aquinas University Parish in Charlottesville, VA, completing that assignment in November 2008. Since January 2009, he has served as Socius and Vicar Provincial of the Province of Saint Joseph in New York City.

My Portion and Cup

You and I cannot respond to God unless God has first called us and chosen us. I am calling this reflection on the Mystery of the Priesthood: "My portion and cup," taken from verse 5 of Psalm 16: *O Lord, it is you who are my portion and cup; it is you yourself who are my prize.* But it seems to me that Psalm 16 is more fitting as *the Priest's own response to having been chosen by God* to be "peculiarly His own". Yet, before we look at our response to having been chosen by God, we should reflect for a moment on the fact of God's choice, because God always takes the initiative.

Anyone who prays the Divine Office regularly is familiar with the passage in the Book of Deuteronomy, Ch. 32 (which we are given for Saturday Morning Prayer – Week II in the Breviary) that says:

> When the Most High assigned the nations their heritage, when he parceled out the descendants of Adam, he set up the boundaries of the peoples after the number of the sons of God; while the Lord's own portion was Jacob, his hereditary share was Israel. [31]

The image here is of God's dividing up the whole world into various sections for all the "descendants of Adam" – "Okay, you go there...and you go there...and you'll stay

---

[31] *The New American Bible* (NAB), Confraternity of Christian Doctrine, Washington, DC, 1970: Deut 32:8-9.

between this river and that mountain range... But this little piece of land, nestled right in the crook of the Fertile Crescent, at the eastern end of the Mediterranean, this I'm keeping for myself. Here I will settle the descendants of my servant Jacob. They shall be My people, and I will be their God."

And we see, at the end of the Book of Numbers, that when God finally settled His Chosen People on the Land He had promised to Abraham and his descendants forever, God went about dividing up the land, apportioning the country among the tribes of Israel, the sons of Jacob, through Moses and Joshua. But the tribe of Levi and the *kohanim* (the descendants of Aaron the Priest), the Priestly class, who had been charged, during the years of wandering in the desert, with encamping around the Tabernacle that contained the Ark, were not given a portion of the Land, from which to draw their sustenance. However, the fact that the tribes of Levi and Simeon were not given their own portion of land (Simeon's land was completely within the territory of the tribe of Judah, and the tribe eventually got absorbed by Judah) was at first a punishment for Levi and Simeon's murdering of Shechem who had defiled their sister Dinah (in Gen 34).[32]

---

[32] In Jacob's "Last Testament" as recorded in the 49th chapter of Genesis, he says that, because of their excess in revenging the rape of their sister Dinah, Levi and Simeon will be "scattered in Israel, dispersed in Jacob," meaning they will have no ancestral territory of their own in the land, but they will live scattered among the others.

Yet when the division of the Promised Land takes place, after the years in the desert, the fact that the sons of Levi get no ancestral land of their own, but rather towns and their surrounding grazing lands scattered throughout the territories of all the other tribes of Israel, has been transformed from what was originally a punishment into God's way of providing especially for the Priests (the *kohanim*) and the Levites, who stood guard and who served the Lord throughout Israel's sojourn in the desert. They are to live off of God's own portion, offered by all the other tribes, as the first-fruits of the harvest and the flock and the herd.

In the Book of Numbers, chapter 18, this is what is promised to the Priests, the sons of Aaron, who were also members of the Tribe of Levi:

> The Lord said to Aaron, "I Myself have given you charge of the contributions made to Me in the various sacred offerings of the Israelites; by perpetual ordinance I have assigned them to you and to your sons as your Priestly share. You shall have the right to share in the oblations that are most sacred, in whatever they offer me as cereal offerings or sin offerings or guilt offerings; these shares shall accrue to you and to your sons. In eating them you shall treat them as most sacred; every male among you may partake of them. As sacred, they belong to you.
>
> You shall also have what is removed from the gift in every wave offering of the Israelites; by perpetual ordinance I have assigned it to you and to your sons and daughters. All in your

family who are clean may partake of it. I have also assigned to you all the best of the new oil and of the new wine and grain that they give to the Lord as their first fruits; and likewise, of whatever grows on their land, the first products that they bring in to the Lord shall be yours; all of your family who are clean may partake of them. Whatever is doomed in Israel shall be yours. Every living thing that opens the womb, whether of man or of beast, such as are to be offered to the Lord, shall be yours; but you must let the first-born of man, as well as of unclean animals, be redeemed.... But the first-born of cattle, sheep or goats shall not be redeemed; they are sacred. Their blood you must splash on the altar and their fat you must burn as a sweet-smelling oblation to the Lord. Their meat, however, shall be yours, just as the breast and the right leg of the wave offering belong to you. By perpetual ordinance I have assigned to you and to your sons and daughters all the contributions from the sacred gifts which the Israelites make to the Lord; this is an inviolable covenant to last forever before the Lord, for you and for your descendants. Then the Lord said to Aaron: "You shall not have any heritage in the land of the Israelites nor hold any portion among them; I will be your portion and your heritage among them.[33]

Now, obviously, these are passages of Scripture that you and I do not regularly meditate upon. We won't find Numbers, Ch. 18 in the Lectionary! And yet in it, we see this intimate connection between the Priest and Levite having "no inheritance in their land," nor "any portion"

---

[33] *NAB*, Num 18:8-15, 17-20.

among them, precisely because God Himself is their "portion and heritage." *You shall not have any heritage in the land of the Israelites nor hold any portion among them; I will be your portion and your heritage among them.*

And this is what God commanded of the Levites, through Moses:

> The Lord said to Moses, "Give the Levites these instructions: When you receive from the Israelites the tithes I have assigned you from them as your heritage, you are to make a contribution from them to the Lord, a tithe of the tithes; and your contribution will be credited to you as if it were grain from the threshing floor or new wine from the press. Thus you too shall make a contribution from all the tithes you receive from the Israelites, handing over to Aaron the Priest the part to be contributed to the Lord. From all the gifts you receive, and from the best parts, you are to consecrate to the Lord your own full contribution...Your families as well as you may eat them anywhere, since they are your recompense for service at the meeting tent. You will incur no guilt so long as you make a contribution of the best part. Do not profane the sacred gifts of Israelites and so bring death on yourselves." [34]

So, all the tribes of Israel had to tithe – to offer a tenth of all they had to the Lord – which would be the special portion for the Priests and Levites, but the Levites, whose task it was to accept the tithes of the people,

---

[34] *NAB*, Num 18:25-29, 31-32.

would then in turn tithe a tenth of everything they received from the people, which would be given to "Aaron the Priest." This would be counted as their tithe, their first-fruits to the Lord, even though they themselves had received it.

Again, if we pray the Divine Office regularly, we are familiar with the canticle from the Prophet Jeremiah, which we sing at Morning Prayer:

> Hear the word of the LORD, O nations
> proclaim it on distant coasts, and say:
> He who scattered Israel, now gathers them together,
> he guards them as a shepherd his flock.
> The LORD shall ransom Jacob,
> he shall redeem him from the hand of his conqueror.
> Shouting, they shall mount the heights of Zion,
> they shall come streaming to the LORD'S blessings:
> The grain, the wine, and the oil,
> the sheep and the oxen;
> They themselves shall be like watered gardens,
> never again shall they languish.
> Then the virgins shall make merry and dance,
> and young men and old as well.
> I will turn their mourning into joy
> I will console and gladden them after their sorrows.
> I will lavish choice portions upon the Priests,
> and my people shall be filled with my blessings,
> says the LORD. 35

The ability to "lavish choice portions upon the Priests" is directly related to the abundance of blessings that God showered upon the whole people, because the "portion of the Priest" was the portion the people returned to the

---

35 *NAB*, Jer 31:10-14.

Lord in thanksgiving for God's providential care of them. It also tied the "fortune" of the Priests and Levites to that of the people in general. If the harvest of the land was small, the portion offered to the Lord was proportionately smaller, as well, though always the best of whatever was produced. If the harvest of the land was great, then the portion offered to the Lord was correspondingly greater.

I think this fact bears some reflecting upon by us, especially in regards to how we live in our own rectories and communities, and the benefits and privileges we enjoy, precisely when compared to those enjoyed by the majority of the people whom we are serving. If the People of God walk into our rectories and go, "Wow!" (as has been known to happen), or if they vie for invitations to our table because they know they'll be eating better than they do in their own homes (which happens quite often!) then somehow I think we've lost that sense of proportion and propriety and good stewardship.

So, now we come back to Psalm 16, from which I took my title of this particular reflection, "My Portion and Cup."

Preserve me, God, I take refuge in you.
I say to the Lord: "You are my God.
My happiness lies in you alone."

He has put into my heart a marvelous love
for the faithful ones who dwell in his land.
Those who choose other gods increase their sorrows.
Never will I offer their offerings of blood.

Never will I take their name upon my lips.

O Lord, it is you who are my portion and cup;
it is you yourself who are my prize.
The lot marked out for me is my delight:
welcome indeed the heritage that falls to me!

I will bless the Lord who gives me counsel,
who even at night directs my heart.
I keep the Lord ever in my sight:
since he is at my right hand, I shall stand firm.

And so my heart rejoices, my soul is glad;
even my body shall rest in safety.
For you will not leave my soul among the dead,
nor let your beloved know decay.

You will show me the path of life,
the fullness of joy in your presence
at your right hand happiness forever. [36]

King David, the traditional author of the Psalm, was, of course, not of the Priestly class. He was of the tribe of Benjamin, not the Tribe of Levi. However, we know that the Office of Priest and King in Israel were very closely linked together, because both the Priest and King were anointed, and both represented the People before the Lord. In the Person of our Lord Jesus Christ, the Son of David, of course, both offices would be united perfectly for all eternity, a "Priest forever, according to the order of Melchizedek." Psalm 16 is a particularly Priestly prayer; a prayer, we could say, of Christ our High Priest, and of course, the Church has read this Psalm from the

---

[36] *The Liturgy of the Hours*, The Catholic Book Publishing Co, New York, 1976.

146

beginning as if coming from the lips of Christ our High Priest, particularly in these verses, *"And so my heart rejoices and my soul is glad; even my body shall rest in safety. For you will not leave my soul among the dead, nor let your beloved know decay."*

"O Lord, it is You are my portion and cup. It is you yourself who are my prize. The lot marked out for me is my delight. Welcome indeed the heritage that falls to me."

Here we see that the Psalmist is not referring primarily to all those "sin offerings and wave offerings" and the first-fruits of the womb and the choice parts of every sacrifice to the Lord that a Priest got to enjoy; no, it is God Himself who is "his portion and cup," his prize, his lot, his heritage. It speaks of an intimacy, a closeness to the Lord that comes, not from being well-provided for materially, but from his Priestly service at the Tabernacle of the Lord.

What this means for us, we who have been called to the service of the Lord, who have been or are seeking to be "ordained to the Priesthood of Jesus Christ, through the Invocation of the Holy Spirit and the Laying on of hands,", we who have discerned a call to serve the Lord at His altar, in His sanctuary, is that we are not *possessors;* there is nothing we can call our own. We are instead *"possessees."*

I use that made-up word, *"possessees,"* instead of "possessions," because you and I are not *things* that can be possessed; we are persons made in the Image and

Likeness of God. We belong entirely to the Lord; we have placed ourselves entirely in His hands, at His disposal. But in exchange, He has promised us an intimacy, a closeness that comes from "dwelling in His tent." It is a difficult thing – but each of us called to the Priesthood, and perhaps to a life of religious consecration as well, must strive to make our own the words of the Psalmist in Psalm 16: *I say to the Lord, "You are my God. My happiness lies in you alone."* In **You** alone. **My** happiness. **Alone**.

What this means is that because we have been called to be "God's own hereditary share, or as God said to Aaron and his descendants, "I am your portion and inheritance," it means that any attempt on our part to make something, anything else "our portion and cup," our inheritance will necessarily end in frustration. In effect, seeking our happiness in something, anything else is almost like stealing from others, taking what does not belong to us. The things of this world belong to the other "tribes." We are called to live on what God chooses to give us, and what He chooses to give is the very best. And it's the very best, *not* as the world judges it, *but simply because it is from God*, because it belongs to Him, and He provides for us from what is His own by right. God won't stop us from trying to fill ourselves with something else (and try all the time we do), yet we are not made for those "things". We are made for God alone. This is what I think it means to live a spirit of radical Gospel poverty – to resist the temptation, day in and day out, to fill our emptiness with anything but God alone, and to say each day, from the midst of our poverty and emptiness: *My happiness lies in you alone. It is you yourself who are my prize. The lot marked out for me is my delight.*

In his letter calling for the "Year for Priests", our Holy Father, Pope Benedict XVI referred to how the Curé of Ars lived the evangelical counsels of poverty, chastity and obedience in a way that was appropriate to his life as a secular Priest. He wrote:

> The Curé of Ars lived the "evangelical counsels" in a way suited to his Priestly state. His poverty was not the poverty of a religious or a monk, but that proper to a Priest: while managing much money (since well-to-do pilgrims naturally took an interest in his charitable works), he realized that everything had been donated to his church, his poor, his orphans, the girls of his "Providence", his families of modest means. Consequently, he "was rich in giving to others and very poor for himself". As he would explain: "My secret is simple: give everything away; hold nothing back". When he lacked money, he would say amiably to the poor who knocked at his door: "Today I'm poor just like you, I'm one of you". At the end of his life, he could say with absolute tranquility: "I no longer have anything. The good Lord can call me whenever He wants!" [37]

---

37 *Letter of His Holiness Pope Benedict XVI Proclaiming a Year for Priest on the 150th Anniversary of the "Dies Natalis" of the Curé of Ars*, Vatican Polyglot Press, 2009.

Or as Job said, *Naked I came forth from my mother's womb, and naked shall I go back again. The LORD gave and the LORD has taken away; blessed be the name of the LORD!*[38] Amen.

[38] *NAB*, Job 1:21

FATHER JAMES RAFFERTY

Ordained in 1994 as a priest of the Diocese of Scranton, Father James Rafferty completed theological studies at the North American College and the Gregorian University in Rome. In addition to parochial ministry, he served as director of religious formation at Sacred Heart Junior/Senior High School and as campus minister at Marywood University. He served on the faculty of Saint Pius X Seminary, a college formation program, and he has been involved with spiritual direction and teaching for the Institute for Priestly Formation in Omaha, Nebraska. Father Rafferty completed doctoral studies in Moral Theology at the Alphonsian Academy in Rome in May 2010. Currently he serves as assistant professor of moral theology and as a formator at Saint Charles Borromeo Seminary in Philadelphia.

Divine Compassion in the Priestly Heart:
A Paschal Presence where the World's Longing Meets God's Faithful Love

While on retreat in Assisi during Holy Week, I had the privilege of concelebrating the Holy Thursday Mass of the Lord's Supper in the Basilica of Saint Clare. The Franciscan who celebrated the liturgy shared a profoundly beautiful homily centered on the shocking, embarrassing, disorienting love of Christ displayed at the Last Supper and in the whole of the paschal mystery. In conversation with the same Franciscan later on, I discovered a brother Priest who exhibited an extraordinary hospitality, a generous availability, and a love for poverty that freed him to follow Christ in humility and gratitude. He appeared to me as a man who had embraced the Franciscan charism with fervor years earlier, and his fidelity to his Franciscan commitment exercised in his daily pattern of life for many years allowed the ideal of Saint Francis to seep into the fibers of his personality. What I noticed and admired about this Franciscan Priest was that he is "all in." Not only had he given himself over to the Franciscan life on the day when he professed his vows, but his daily surrender of himself year after year made the Franciscan rule second nature for him. He lived the charism of Francis deeply, spontaneously, in an almost unconscious way. The encounter with this Priest who radiated the love of Saint Francis stirred in my heart the question, "When a man lives the diocesan Priestly vocation in generous self-offering year after year, when he is "all in," what qualities does he take on from the repeated surrender to the grace of his Priestly commitment?" Stated another way, I wondered, "How is Christ's own love refracted through the humanity of a diocesan Priest as he permits the Holy Spirit to claim more and more of his life in ordained ministry?"

One who has obviously lived into the grace of the diocesan Priestly vocation and allowed the Priestly character to penetrate his whole life and personality is Saint John Vianney. John Vianney was renowned for his prayerfulness, his devotion to Mary, his ascetical discipline, his reverent love for Priesthood, and his tireless service to his parish, but the characteristics that most attracted others to him were his zeal in the confessional and in the pulpit. John Vianney famously dedicated many hours each day to the sacrament of reconciliation. As a minister of God's sacramental mercy, John witnessed to the Father's divine compassion healing wounds and dispelling darkness. Enormous crowds also gathered in Ars to hear John preach. In his homilies and catechesis, John broke open the mystery of divine love revealed in the cross and resurrection of Jesus Christ. The concrete details of John's life testify to the Trinity's steadfast love and mercy. Unquestionably, John Vianney, the parish Priest of Ars, was "all in." When people encountered John, they recognized in him the Father's tender love, the same compassion that people beheld in Jesus' eyes and in Jesus' voice and in Jesus' touch during his public ministry. John Vianney models a Priestly life that continues to be affected by the Holy Spirit long after the day of ordination. John lived into the gift of Priesthood ever more generously until the Priestly character consumed his personality.

John Vianney reveals a particular way of understanding the diocesan Priesthood. Certainly all ordained Priests share the privilege of celebrating the Church's sacraments, but it seems that diocesan Priests especially are servants of the sacramental life of the Church. For religious Priests, the celebration of the sacramental rites occurs within the unique charism or specific mission of the religious community. Many different religious orders support parishes where religious Priests engage in ministry much the same way in which their brother diocesan Priests serve in neighboring parishes. However, for the diocesan Priest, sacramental ministry occupies a priority that is not so intrinsic to Priests who belong to religious communities. The specific mission of diocesan Priesthood involves making the sacraments available to the faithful because the diocesan Priest directly participates in the diocesan Bishop's responsibility to lead, teach, and sanctify. While religious Priests may collaborate in this pastoral mandate, the diocesan vocation more distinctly binds the Priest to his local Bishop and the care of souls in the local church.

It appears, then, that the diocesan Priest, as servant of the Church's sacramental life, also may be described as the custodian of the Church's epiclesis, for the Priest alone offers the epicletic prayer at the center of each sacramental liturgy. For example, in the celebration of the Mass during the Eucharistic Prayer, the Priest calls out on behalf of the gathered assembly for the Father to send the Holy Spirit to transform the offerings of bread and wine into the sacred Body and Blood of Jesus Christ. The Priestly role in the Eucharistic liturgy includes this prayer that expresses the community's longing for Christ to be present among them. The epiclesis verbalizes the whole community's hunger to receive Jesus and the powerlessness to meet him without the gift of the Spirit from the Father. In the mystery of the Church's life by God's design, the Priest has been entrusted with this responsibility to offer the people's cry with his own for the outpouring of the Spirit, who gives life in abundance. All the baptized exercise a holy and effective epiclesis each time they offer a prayer of petition to God. The Priest, though, cries out in the sacramental rituals in a petition for the Holy Spirit in a manner not shared by all the faithful. The prayer of the baptized lay person does not transform bread and wine into the Body and Blood of Jesus, nor does the petition of the non-ordained absolve sin. This distinction grounds the Priest's humility, for he knows well in his heart that he himself does not possess the power to transform bread into Christ's Body, nor does he remove sin by his own authority. Instead, the Priestly role charges the ordained with asking these particular blessings of God for others. The Priest offers the prayer that begs God's grace to transform the lives of those around him. In sacramental liturgies the Priest functions as the mouthpiece of the faithful's cry for salvation, for the transforming presence of the Spirit who raised Christ from the dead. The Priest exercises his ministry at the service of people's longing for redemption.

As unique bearer of the Church's power of epiclesis, the Priest ought to be at home within the suffering of the world. Rather than interceding from a comfortable distance of detached safety, the Priestly office impels the ordained to be present among the places where the wounded and the sinner wait to meet God's steadfast love. In communion with the divine compassion of Jesus Christ, indeed possessed by this self-offering love of the Savior, the Priest ought to desire deeply to remain close to the poverty of his brothers and sisters, which, of course, only mirrors his own poverty. As a result of this epicletic posture maintained over decades of Priestly service, the Priest's heart becomes increasingly vulnerable as it hosts Christ's own tenderness for the sick, the lost, and the abandoned. The mission of the faithful pastor unites him to his people right at the point of imperfection and weakness, pain and sorrow, instead of seeking some idealistic plateau untouched by human misery. Likewise, the Priest rejects the impulse to fix other people's lives, a drive which only manifests a fearful intolerance of suffering. Rather, the Priest stands amid human anguish, like Jesus, as icon of the Father's merciful heart, and because the Priest knows the Trinity's unbounded love himself, he can call out from the darkest, most tragic human circumstances not with despair but with the confidence of the Father's unhesitating response to his children's cry. "For I have put my hope in the Everlasting to save you, and joy has come to me from the Holy One, because of the mercy which soon will come to you from your everlasting Savior" (Baruch 4:22). In this regard, the Priest shares a deep bond with Mary, who remained with Jesus in adoring love, whether at the joyful celebration of marriage at Cana or at the agony of Calvary. The Priestly epicletic prayer repeatedly proclaims the scandalous fact that God plunges into the tomb of humanity's suffering.

While the Priest raises the cry for salvation on behalf of the burdened and the bound, the Priest also witnesses the unimagined outpouring of grace that flows from the pierced side of the glorified Christ. In this way, the Priest truly bridges the everyday world and the world of grace. That is, the Priest is present to the daily miracles that occur when, in response to the Church's petition, the Father pours out his love in the abundance of the Holy Spirit. The Priest's ministry situates him in the space of the resurrection. As bearer of the epicletic prayer, the Priest is intimately familiar with the longing of men and women for divine intervention, but he is also privileged witness of God's fidelity to his people. The Priest knows the horrible grief of the tomb, but he also beholds the radiance of Easter. In the sacrament of Reconciliation, for example, he sees the sinner's heart, closed in upon itself, burst open as living sign of the empty tomb. The Priest is not only messenger of hope in the form of prayerful intercession; he also announces the fulfillment of hope because he testifies to the Trinity's ongoing transfiguration of the world in which we live. The Priest lives in humanity's thirst for union with God and in God's thirst for union with his children. He shares, too, in the joyful moment of recognition when Love gazes upon the beloved, and the beloved welcomes the gaze of Love to the very depths of one's being. The Priest inhabits the heart of the Trinity, where infinite compassion bursts forth in the new creation. In a particular way, the Priest, as he perceives the mystery of divine love reaching out to touch sorrow and pain, experiences a personal communion with the Sacred Heart of Jesus. The Priest glimpses the astounding mystery of the Savior's pierced heart, and he allows this eternal fire of mercy to dwell in his own heart. He is made aware each day that the Father hears the cry of his children and that God responds by offering himself unreservedly. In this way, the Priest touches the whole grandeur of the paschal mystery in his own Priestly service: at the altar, in the confessional, in the hospital, among families, and in the parish office. The same glorified Christ whom the Priest meets in the solitude of contemplation waits to meet him in all the varied experiences of ministry, where the Risen Lord continues to impart peace and to reveal himself by the wounds he bears (John 20:19-20).

In my own Priesthood, I marvel at the patient love with which the Father guides me toward greater maturity as a Priest. I have been enthralled with Priesthood from the day of ordination, but I did not always appreciate the power and the privilege of exercising epiclesis on behalf of the Church, and I am still learning how to remain close to Christ's Sacred Heart through the grace of the Holy Spirit. Early in my Priestly service I often felt overwhelmed by the problems of people who turned to the parish Priest for help. Amid the inexpressible wonder of the communion of love in which the Priest serves, I still clung to the misconception that I had to resolve crises or that I should have ready answers for difficult situations. Unfortunately, I did not instinctively point people to Jesus as the sole source of hope and healing, and I was not swift in putting words to the prayer in their hearts. In particular, I wanted to pull back from instances where my heart was stirred to grief as others shared their woundedness. To my regret, there was in me an unacknowledged desire to be a detached practitioner to whom people could turn for comfort or guidance but who could also remain unaffected by the burdens others carried. I recognize how at that time I was reluctant to welcome the Lord immediately into places of suffering – others' or my own. Instead of offering the spontaneous, trusting cry of a son to his Father, I tried to figure out and think through the problems or sorrows people shared with their Priest. I had a deep desire to serve others and good intentions, but I was not embracing the poverty of my own Priesthood, nor was I resting fully in the intimacy Jesus experienced with the Father. I tried too much to do it on my own, and in this way I was not "all in."

I am gratefully aware that the Lord has continued to draw me closer to his heart and so to release more of my Priesthood from my own self-preoccupations. The Father has led me to appreciate my poverty as a Priest as I realize in humility that every aspect of my ministry as a Priest is gift of the Father and place of intimate communion with Jesus in Mary's presence. I have learned by grace to renounce self-reliance and to depend confidently on the Father, who always heeds the prayers of his children. As I embrace the healing power of Priestly prayer, I am more open to witness the miracles of loving mercy that God works each day in people's lives and in my own. I exercise Priesthood now with greater humility and awe. Truly I live a Priesthood that I do not deserve. The experience of growing in comfort and confidence as a servant of the Church's epiclesis has opened my spirit to the joy of a Priestly life that is beyond me. When I am honest about how little I can do myself, then I am capable of acknowledging the magnificent works that the Lord is doing in everyday life. Most importantly, I am peaceful in walking with others in their frailty or their anguish because I know how desperately the Lord wants to console. As I live more consciously from my own sonship before the Father, I am learning how to exercise a Priesthood based on prayerful intercession that accomplishes more than I can do. My Priestly life has become much more intensely a dialogue of love and desire with the Trinity, and I am becoming slowly shaped by the Sacred Heart of Jesus as I permit myself to remain close to his divine compassion.

Bishop Edward M. Rice

Bishop Edward M. Rice was ordained on January 3, 1987 and was sent to his first Priestly assignment, Our Lady of the Presentation Parish, in Overland, MO (1987-1991). In 1991, he was assigned to teach at Saint Mary's High School while residing at Saint Mary Magadalen Parish. In 1994, Monsignor Rice was also appointed Assistant Director of Cardinal Glennon College Seminary. The following year he was appointed Director of the College, a position he held until June 2000 when he was appointed Pastor of Saint John the Baptist Parish in south Saint Louis. In June of 2008, Archbishop Burke appointed Monsignor Rice as the Designate Vocation Director. He assumed full duties as Vocation Director of the Archdiocese of Saint Louis on August 1, 2008. He was ordained a Bishop on January 13, 2011.[39]

---

[39] Bishop Edward M. Rice was named Auxiliary Bishop of the Archdiocese of Saint Louis after having written this reflection.

Like No Other

In one way, it was a day like any other day. I started in front of the Blessed Sacrament, making my daily Holy Hour prior to the early Mass in the parish church. Then off to another parish for an 8 am Vocation Mass and talk with the elementary students. By mid-morning, I was back in my car on the way to the office for a meeting with youth ministers. After lunch, I was off with my office staff to scope out a new location for our summer vocation weekend for girls. After a four mile run, I was showered and ready for 4:15 PM Evening Prayer. As Apostolic Coordinator for the junior class of Cardinal Glennon College Seminary, I accompanied the seminarians to the local soup kitchen. By 6:30 PM, I was back at the seminary for supper and some serious desk time returning phone calls and e-mails. It's Tuesday, which means we have overnight Adoration of the Blessed Sacrament at the parish where I am in residence, Our Holy Redeemer Catholic Church in suburban Saint Louis, MO. On Tuesdays I try to leave the office early and end my day as I began, in front of the Blessed Sacrament. As I knelt before the Blessed Sacrament that evening I was ready to call it a day, or so I thought.

There was no siren. But the red lights from the ambulance danced through the stained glass windows of the Church, directing my attention away from the

Blessed Sacrament toward the apartment complex directly across the street from the parish where many of the residents are parishioners. No, my day was not finished. As I ran across the street, I immediately questioned why I did not just grab the Oil of the Sick in the first place. The odds were good that whatever the emergency, a parishioner was involved. And so it was! After a quick run back to the sacristy for the Oil of the Sick, I was back in the apartment of one of our parishioners to anoint her before she was placed in the ambulance. Finally back in the pew to finish my late evening Holy Hour, an intense joy swelled in my heart as I realized how God had used me in such an unexpected way. Just when I was ready to put the day to an end, the Good Lord saw fit for me to celebrate one last sacrament. What a joy! What began as a typical day became a day like no other!

As I write the details of this experience, I realize that any Priest who may read this account could offer the details of his own day. What Priest could not identify with this – and more! Gazing upon the Blessed Sacrament exposed on the altar, I realized that I had moved from an encounter with the Lord in the Blessed Sacrament to an encounter with the Lord in a sick and needy parishioner. I had moved from the altar of sacrifice to the altar of service. And I was once again reminded of one of the beautiful and profound meanings of the Priesthood; all that a Priest does in the course of his day is actually an extension of what he celebrates in the Holy Sacrifice of the Mass. The great French theologian, Lacordaire, said it so well, "In the morning, at Mass, I am the Priest and Christ is the victim. The rest of the day, Christ is the Priest and I am the victim." That daily ascent to the altar, offering the Holy Sacrifice, and the descent from the altar to the various activities of the day, gives profound meaning to the ministry of the Priest.

As a young child receiving the Sacrament of Confirmation, I took the name "John" simply because it was the name of my brother who happened to be my sponsor. I had no thought of Saint John the Baptist, Saint John of the Cross or Saint John the Apostle and Evangelist. Years later, as I approached ordination, I made a conscious choice to claim Saint John the Evangelist as my Confirmation name. Why? Well, it was Saint John who sat next to Our Lord at the Last Supper and in that most intimate moment heard the beating of Our Lord's Sacred Heart, a heart filled with love for us. Next, it was Saint John who stood with Mary at the foot of the cross, the same cross that symbolizes the unconditional love of the Heart of Christ. Saint John, therefore stands at two pivotal moments in the life of Christ, moments which define the Priesthood.

Artists through the centuries have tried to portray the intimacy of that moment, solemn, mystical and intimate. And yet, for all its beauty, that moment is also tainted. Judas is there as well and Satan has entered his heart. The contrast could not be more dramatic!

Saint John approaches and chooses the Heart of Christ, while Judas chooses to allow Satan to fill his heart. The Upper Room was filled with contrasting emotions at that moment. Choices have been made, alliances established, hearts have been exposed.

At every Mass offered we become that Beloved Disciple John. And like John, we are given the opportunity to recline next to Our Lord and unite ourselves to His Sacred Heart. As we rest in that Heart, Our Lord offers Himself in His Body and Blood. In that great act of offering, He fulfills our deepest longings. We are given the opportunity to share in that one, perfect sacrifice of praise. And in that moment, we experience a union just as profound as the experience of Saint John in the Upper Room.

Each Mass becomes a unique encounter like no other. From this encounter, we receive the strength to move, like Saint John, and take our place at the foot of the cross, the other defining moment in the Priesthood. The tender, sorrowful emotion of this moment too has been portrayed through the centuries. It is impossible to calculate how many churches depict Mary and John at the foot of the Cross. One cannot help but be touched by the scene. And in the exchange between Our Lord and Saint John, the care of the Blessed Mother is given to him and to the Church. And so again, to us Priests, we are given the charge to care for the Church and to be concerned for the care of souls.

Our Priestly ministry, as marred as it may be, should always flow between these two defining moments – the Upper Room and the foot of Calvary. The Cross, the Eucharist, the Paschal Mystery is the source of strength for all we do. Teaching in the classroom, marriage preparation, funerals, bids for tuck pointing or gutter work; whatever our day looks like, and each day is like no other, all flows from being that "beloved disciple" who reclines close to Him, and then in the varied opportunities in Priestly ministry moves the Priest to the foot of the Cross. This movement becomes a beautiful pilgrimage, a daily pilgrimage, back and forth from the Upper Room to Calvary. And in this daily pilgrimage, there is an exchange of love. Again, "In the morning at Mass I am the Priest and Christ is the victim. The rest of the day Christ is the Priest and I am the victim."

This pilgrimage, this constant movement between the Upper Room and Calvary, also becomes an opportunity to examine the events and activities of the day in light of these beautiful moments. Pope John Paul II, in *Pastores Dabo Vobis*, challenged seminarians (and therefore Priests) to reject whatever is contrary to their vocation. If we are truly living out the Priestly life according to the theology and discipline of the Church, then I am called to reject whatever does not fall within the path of the Upper Room and Calvary. I must be honest in scrutinizing my daily activities and reject whatever pulls me away from the intimacy Jesus desires to have with me. I must reject whatever would distance me from the shadow of the Cross. The noble and lofty understanding of "Priest" as *alter Christus* demands that I look at my daily actions, whether in my nightly examination of conscience, morning Holy Hour, a day of recollection or yearly retreat, all with a discerning eye. In the Catechism of the Catholic Church, we are reminded that through the Priesthood of Jesus Christ, the presence of Christ is made visible(CCC, 1549). Such a lofty understanding demands constant reflection and examination in light of the daily activities of the individual Priest. How often we are reminded in the ordination ritual that we act not alone. No, each Priest is a "co-worker" with the Bishop since he has been configured to Christ and acts in the person of Christ the head. The Priesthood of Jesus Christ is like no other. It demands the highest virtue, the strongest virtue, the greatest diligence in life so that one never strays from the path between the Upper Room and Calvary. We must safeguard our Priesthood and live by the highest ideals of Christ our High Priest, even as we are weak and sinful vessels.

In *Journal of a Soul*, the autobiography of Pope John XXIII, I gained a most profound and lasting insight. When you read his work, you gain a window into the simple joys and struggles of his Priesthood. The reflections of Pope John XXIII could be the reflections of any Priest. As a Churchman, Bishop and Priest, he shared the same Priesthood that all Priests share, the eternal Priesthood of Christ. In reading his autobiography, you gain a sense of the man himself, a sense that he was never satisfied with himself. He was always driven to do more, to give more, to further the cause of the Church. He loved the Church, whether in his early years as secretary, or spiritual director at the seminary or as Papal Ambassador to foreign countries. He was never satisfied. He always pushed himself to give more, and again, all to further the cause of the Church he loved so much.

He certainly did not have an inflated sense of himself. No, the humility of the man flows forth from his reflections, a humility coupled with zeal and simplicity. "I must always look upon myself as a servant. Therefore I shall have not one single moment free for serving my own interests..." And yet he goes on to say, "So much pride and arrogance and presumption, and I do not even know how to be a servant." Here we see his great and lofty desires, and yet the frail, human side of his Priesthood. In 1950, looking back on 25 years as a Bishop and 46 years of Priestly ordination he wrote, "Twenty-five years of Episcopal Masses, offered with all the splendor of good intentions, and all the dust of the road, oh, what a mystery of mingled grace and shame." A mystery of grace and shame! Those are the words he chose to summarize his twenty-five years as a Bishop of the Church. Would not every Priest describe his Priesthood in the same way? Many volumes have been written about the Priesthood over the past 2,000 year history of the Church, but the Priesthood is lived out in the heart of each individual man. Saint Ambrose too offers valuable insight:

> A Priest is a man and therefore remains fallible and capable of making mistakes. But this does not prevent him from being the anointed of the Lord, marked forever with an indelible sign and having the power to consecrate the Body of Christ.

Pope John XXIII lived out the mystery of the Priesthood with grace and shame and so also for every Priest. Each one of us can identify those moments when we were carried by grace. Being at the right place at the right time, preaching a homily that touched someone's heart, being used by God at just the right moment – it is grace! And, our shame should be before us as well. There is a great wisdom in praying Psalm 51 every Friday, "My offenses, truly I know them, my sin is always before me…what is evil in your sight I have done." Pope John XXIII, quoting the Imitation of Christ, reminds us of the importance of knowing self, our gifts and talents, our weakness and sin, "A humble knowledge of yourself is a surer way to God than profound learning."

Saint John the Apostle, in his 1st letter, chapter 2, challenges us to have no love for the world, what he refers to as the "life of empty show." Why would he say such a thing about the beautiful world created by Almighty God? Because Saint John had encountered love itself, pure love, in the person of Jesus Christ. How could he settle for less? The letter, written around 90 to 100 AD, was some 60 – 70 years after John had reclined at table with the Lord. And that moment was still so powerful for Saint John, it defined him to such an extent that he could say that the things of this world are nothing.

I began this reflection on the Priesthood by describing a day like no other. As I look back, I realize that this experience is the common denominator that unites all Priests as they strive daily to give themselves over to what the Priesthood calls them to – living the love of the heart of Jesus, living a life of selfless service. Indeed, the Priesthood is a life like no other.

Justin Cardinal Rigali

Justin Cardinal Rigali was born in Los Angeles on April 19, 1935, one of seven children born to Henry Alphonsus Rigali and Frances Irene White. He attended Catholic schools in Los Angeles and studied in the archdiocesan seminaries at Los Angeles College, Our Lady Queen of Angels Seminary in San Fernando and Saint John's College and Saint John's Seminary in Camarillo, California. He was ordained a Priest by Cardinal James Francis McIntyre in the Cathedral of Saint Vibiana in Los Angeles on April 25, 1961.

In October 1961, he entered the graduate division of the North American College in Rome and began graduate studies in canon law at the Pontifical Gregorian University. He obtained a doctorate in Canon Law from that university in 1964. From 1964 to 1966, he followed the course of studies at the Pontifical Ecclesiastical Academy, while serving in the English-language section of the Secretariat of State of the Vatican.

From September 1966 to February 1970, he served at the Apostolic Nunciature in Madagascar, which also was the Apostolic Delegation for the islands of Mauritius and La Reunión. During this time in July 1967, he was named a Papal Chamberlain (Monsignor) to His Holiness Pope Paul VI.

In February 1970, Monsignor Rigali became the director of the English-language section of the Vatican

Secretariat of State, and the English-language translator for Pope Paul VI, whom he accompanied to various countries. Monsignor Rigali served as a professor at the Pontifical Ecclesiastical Academy in Rome from 1972 to 1973.

During his service at the Vatican Secretariat of State, he also accompanied Pope John Paul II on a number of international pastoral visits, including the Holy Father's first two major journeys to the United States in 1979 and 1987. The 1979 trip included a visit to Philadelphia. On April 19, 1980 he was named a Prelate of Honor of His Holiness. He became a magistral chaplain in the Knights of Malta on October 25, 1984. On October 13, 1986, he became a Knight of the Holy Sepulchre.

On June 8, 1985, he was named President of the Pontifical Ecclesiastical Academy and Titular Archbishop of Bolsena. Pope John Paul II ordained him to the Episcopacy on September 14, 1985 in the Cathedral of Albano.

From 1985 to 1990, in addition to being President of the Pontifical Ecclesiastical Academy, he held a number of positions at the Vatican, serving the Secretariat of State, the Council for the Public Affairs of the Church, the Congregation for Bishops and the Pontifical Council for the Laity. On December 21, 1989, he was named Secretary of the Congregation for Bishops and on January 2, 1990 he became the Secretary of the College of Cardinals. During the same time, he was also engaged in pastoral services to a number of parishes and seminaries in Rome.

On January 25, 1994, Pope John Paul II appointed him the eighth Bishop and seventh Archbishop of St. Louis. He was formally installed on March 15, 1994 by His Eminence Cardinal Bernardin Gantin, Prefect of the Congregation for Bishops. He received the Pallium from the Holy Father on June 29, 1994.

On July 15, 2003, Pope John Paul II appointed Archbishop Rigali as the twelfth Bishop and eighth Archbishop of Philadelphia. He was named a Cardinal on September 28, 2003. On October 7, 2003, he was installed Archbishop of Philadelphia by Archbishop Gabriel Montalvo, the Apostolic Nuncio, in the Cathedral Basilica of Saints Peter and Paul.

Cardinal Rigali is the spiritual leader of almost 1.5 million Catholics in the City of Philadelphia and the surrounding counties of Bucks, Chester, Delaware, and Montgomery. He is also a successor of Saint John Nepomucene Neumann, the fourth Bishop of Philadelphia (1852-1860) and the first canonized male American saint.

Two weeks after his installation as Archbishop of Philadelphia, he was formally created a Cardinal by Pope John Paul II in the Public Consistory in Saint Peter's Square on October 21, 2003. He was assigned the Titular Church of Saint Prisca in Rome.

The Love of Christ's Heart Explains the Priest's Life

The solemnity of the Sacred Heart that we celebrate year after year is very important for all of us. It is a special moment in the liturgical year of the Church.

Since the beginning of the Church's year, we celebrate *so many different aspects of the mysteries of Christ.* On the feast of the Annunciation we proclaim God's plan of *the Incarnation* of His Son – how the eternal Son of God took on our humanity in the womb of the Virgin Mary and became one of us. In Advent we prepare for Christ's coming. At Christmas we celebrate *the birth of Jesus* in Bethlehem. We adore the Child: true God and true man.

Then we reflect on the events of His hidden and public life, leading up to *His Paschal Mystery*: His Passion, Death and Resurrection. We prolong the celebration of Christ's Resurrection throughout Eastertime, rejoicing at the feast of *His Ascension* into heaven.

Then comes *Pentecost* – full of meaning for us: the sending of the Holy Spirit upon the Apostles, the beginning of the Church's mission with the temporal extension of the Incarnation in the Body of Christ. After Pentecost, those beautiful feasts: the solemnity of *the Most Blessed Trinity* which speaks to us not only about the life of God but also about how the unity of the Church reflects the communion of the love of the Father and the Son in the Holy Spirit. Then we celebrate *Corpus Christi*: the feast of the Body and Blood of Jesus Christ, which in the Eucharist becomes our food and drink.

Symbol of Love and Sign of Life

And finally, we have, the feast of the Sacred Heart of Jesus. It is the feast of *the Incarnate Word* of God, the Son of God, *manifesting His love for us and showing us His Heart as a sign of that love*. But the love that He shows us is none other than the love that He has received from His Father. Remember His words: "As the Father has loved me, so I also love you"(John 15:9).

The feast of the Sacred Heart therefore embraces the love of the Father – the One who so loved the world that He sent His only begotten Son into the world to redeem the world. With a human heart, Christ loves both *His Father* and all those who, through His Incarnation, have become *His brothers and sisters in humanity*.

The Heart that Christ shows us is His living human Heart – united to His living humanity. It is a symbol of His love. But even more it is *the sign of His life*, because the living Heart sustains His human life. And *in God, life and love are identical*.

The love that inspired the Son of God to become man is the same love that inspired Him to die so as to destroy our death, and to rise so as to restore us to life. The love of God explains why Christ came into the world, why He died and rose from the dead, why He set up the Church and sent the Holy Spirit, the Spirit of Love, to be with us forever.

The love of Christ's Heart explains the Eucharist, the living memorial of Christ's Passion, Death and Resurrection. And what is also so clear for us is that *the love of Christ's Heart also explains the great gift and mystery of the Priesthood.*

When Pope John Paul II went to Saint Louis in 1999, he spoke about the merciful love of God that passes through the Heart of Jesus Christ. *The merciful love* of God that passes through the Heart of Jesus Christ is *the cause of the Priesthood.* And the Priesthood is given so that the gift and mystery of Christ's love can be perpetuated in a very special way in the Church.

A Specific Service of Love

The ministerial Priesthood exists so that *a specific service of love* may be exercised in the Church. What is this specific service? It is *the celebration of the Eucharist* and the gathering of a community around an altar to praise God through Jesus Christ, the great High Priest. It is He, Jesus Christ, whom Priests represent and sacramentally make present.

Through the Priesthood, the merciful love of God is also poured out *in the Sacrament of Penance,* through which Jesus Christ continues to forgive sins and to bring humanity into the merciful and compassionate embrace of His Father.

And in numerous other ways too, *Priests mediate the love of Christ to others* through their own humanity. The heart of a Priest, which gives life to his humanity, when united to the heart of Christ, is truly a sign of all his pastoral love for the People of God.

Priests of Jesus Christ are men of service, but their greatest service to the community is *to offer Mass for the living and the dead.* Vatican II teaches us that the pastoral love that Priests have for the people "flows mainly from the Eucharistic Sacrifice which is therefore the center and root of the whole Priestly life"(*Prebyterorum Ordinis,* 14).

The love of Jesus Christ explains His life and it is the reason for the Eucharistic Sacrifice. This love also explains the Priest's life. It is the reason he celebrates the Eucharist, the reason he gives his life in Priestly service and in consecrated celibacy.

Mary, the Mother of Jesus, supported the apostles by her maternal love. May she help all Priests to understand and live *their vocation of Priestly love,* which links them ever more closely to the love of God that passes through the Heart of Jesus Christ.

Father Paul Scalia

Father Paul Scalia was born December 26, 1970 in Charlottesville, Virginia. On October 5, 1995 he was ordained a Deacon at Saint Peter's Basilica, Vatican City-State. On May 18, 1996 he was ordained a priest at Saint Thomas More Cathedral in Arlington, Virginia.

He received his BA from the College of the Holy Cross in Worcester, MA., in 1992, his STB from Pontifical Gregorian University in Rome in 1995, and his MA from the Pontifical University of Saint Thomas Aquinas in Rome in 1996.

Father Scalia is the founder, editor and publisher of The Fenwick Review at the College of Holy Cross. He has written the following: This Rock, Human Life Review, Religion and Liberty, Adoremus Bulletin, First Things, and articles for the Arlington Catholic Herald.

His assignments have been: Parochial Vicar, Saint Bernadette Catholic Church in Springfield, VA; Parochial Vicar, Saint Patrick Catholic Church in Fredericksburg, VA.; Parochial Vicar, Saint Rita Catholic Church, Alexandria, VA.; and was made Parochial Administrator of Saint John the Beloved in July 2008 and Pastor in July 2009.

The Highest Form of Flattery

The newly ordained Priest kneels before the Bishop. A deacon brings the paten and chalice, already prepared with the bread and wine for Mass. The Bishop places the vessels and gifts in the hands of the Priest and says, "Receive the oblation of the holy people, to be offered to God. Understand what you do, imitate what you celebrate, and conform your life to the mystery of the Lord's cross."

This exchange, not even essential to the Sacrament, is one of the most powerful and significant moments of the rite. At that moment the Priest takes as his own the instruments of his ministry – the tools of his trade, as it were. He holds the very things that will shape his life from that day forward. The Bishop's words are powerful indeed. But one phrase in particular stands out: *Imitate what you celebrate.* Those words can serve as the hermeneutic, the interpretive principle, for a Priest's entire life and ministry.

Imitate what you celebrate. Broadly speaking, these words require the Priest to imitate Christ's Sacrifice, which by his sacred powers he makes present at Mass. Hence also the command, "[C]onform your life to the mystery of the Lord's cross." Obviously, a Priest must regard the offering of Mass as the most important aspect of his life and of every day of his life. It is not to be just one of many things that a Priest does but the guiding and unifying principle for all of them. He ought to interpret and approach all other works through that lens.

But the command given on the day of ordination indicates that the Mass has centrality not just as a means of grace but also as a *model* of how to live a Priestly life. *Imitate what you celebrate.* It is significant that the Priest hears these words as he holds the paten and chalice, the bread and wine. It is not just Christ's Sacrifice in general that the Priest must imitate but that Sacrifice as made present in a particular way – as found in the sacred mysteries, in the *liturgical offering* and the *sacramental presence* of His Body and Blood. His imitation must follow the liturgy. Not just the inward, unseen reality of sacrifice and grace but also the outward, tangible manner of offering Mass.

To appreciate the Church's command to Priests, we should cultivate (or recover) an appreciation for the Eucharistic accidents. We know that after the words of consecration bread and wine no longer remain. There is only the Body, Blood, Soul, and Divinity of our Lord. Nevertheless, the *properties* of bread and wine remain. Christ is present *through* the form of bread and wine. Now, the fact that these accidents remain indicates that the form of bread and wine still retain some importance. The form of bread and wine are what theologians call accidentals. But that does not make them incidentals. They still have significance.

The bread and wine signify something not immediately obvious to us: *sacrifice*. Perhaps we do not see this because we sacrifice so little in order to obtain ordinary bread and wine. We do not have to go through the long labor of sowing, harvesting, sifting, crushing, baking, fermenting, etc. It is done for us. We merely get in the car, drive around the corner, grab the loaf or bottle off the shelf and put down relatively little money – perhaps even by the convenience of a debit or credit card.

Modern conveniences blind us to the sacrifice necessary for normal bread and wine. For wheat to become bread and for grapes to become wine, there is a death involved. The wheat must be harvested, sifted, ground, then subjected to fire to become bread. The grapes must be cut down in their prime, and then crushed to release their interior life. Only by dying this death can wheat and grapes become the necessary matter for the Eucharist. Thus even in the order of nature the Eucharist comes to us through sacrifice – through the millstone and winepress, through mortification and death. Without this there can be no bread and wine – and therefore no Eucharist.

So also the Priest: *Imitate what you celebrate.* As he hears these words the Priest holds bread and wine. To imitate what he celebrates the Priest must become like what he holds – like wheat and grapes become bread and wine. He must surrender his life to be sacrificed – to be cut down, sifted, crushed, ground, placed in the fire. He must not only offer sacrifice; he must *be* sacrificed.

Saint Ignatius of Antioch understood this well. En route to his martyrdom, he wrote to the Romans, "I am God's wheat and I shall be ground by the teeth of beasts, that I may become the pure bread of Christ." These words had particular meaning for Saint Ignatius, who was in fact torn to pieces by lions. But his words have significance for all Priests. In the service of Christ and the Church, Priests must be ground to become the pure bread of Christ. *Imitate what you celebrate.* Saint Ignatius's millstone was the lions. The millstone for a Priest today will undoubtedly be different. But his willingness to submit to it must be the same.

To the degree a Priest abandons himself to the millstone – to the daily grind, we might say – to that degree he will live his Priesthood. To the degree a Priest embraces the sacrifices asked of him – the tasks, challenges, setbacks, the demands on his time, energy and talents, the demands on his heart most of all – to that degree he will live his Priesthood. To the degree he resists sacrifice and creates all sorts of ways to avoid it – to that degree he not only fails to live his Priesthood...he betrays it.

Imagine wheat and grapes rebelling against the hand of the harvester and vinedresser. They would never realize their proper end of becoming bread and wine and the even more glorious end of becoming the Eucharist. They must allow themselves to be cut down – and in their prime! – in order to become bread and wine, and then to become the Eucharist. But the rebellion of wheat and grapes would be less shocking than the resistance of the Priest to the hand of the Divine Harvester and Vinedresser. Because it is more in the nature of a Priest to be sacrificed than of wheat and grapes. Not all wheat makes it to bread and to the altar, not all grapes to wine. But every Priest is ordained not only to sacrifice but also to be sacrificed. Not only to spend but to be spent (cf. 2 Cor 12:15).

Imitate what you celebrate. Monsignor Ronald Knox gives us another way to understand this hermeneutic for Priestly life. He describes the Sacred Host, the Real Presence of Christ under the form of bread, as "the window in the wall." A window is part of a wall. But at the same time, a window gives us a view and a certain access to what is beyond the wall. A window introduces us to the outside that we cannot otherwise see. So also the Host. Retaining the form of bread, the Host remains part of this world – but as the Real Presence of Jesus, the Host gives us a view of the next world, indeed of Christ Himself. Thus, when we look at the Sacred Host we look upon the properties of bread which give us entrance – as a window does – to something beyond us, beyond this world into heaven, beyond time into eternity, to Christ Himself.

The window in the wall. Perhaps we can hear in that phrase an apt description of a Priest. Now, a Priest is not the window in the wall in the same sense as the

Eucharist. He is *not* the Real Presence of our Lord (no matter how highly he might think of himself!). And yet if he is to imitate what he celebrates, then he must approximate this truth: he must be in this world and yet provide an opening to the next.

Like a window, he is part of this world. Ordination does not undo or eliminate his human nature. He does not become an angel (God knows!). Nevertheless, the Priest stands as a window. While remaining a man and among men, he himself ought to provide a view, a glimpse, a certain access to things unseen, to truths beyond this world. By his conduct he ought to manifest what the eye cannot see. Looking at him, who although ordained still remains a man, a part of creation, the faithful should have access to something greater.

It is never right to say of a Priest (as we hear so often in response to scandals), "Well, he's only human." First, this does a disservice to our human nature – as if being human excuses immorality and, worse, as if immorality makes us human. Further, the Priest, although human, is not *only* human. He has been entrusted, in his very being, with something divine. People have a right to expect something more of a Priest – that something of heaven be seen through this window, that his life, bearing, and conversation direct us to what is above. That he reveal something of Christ Himself. Our Lord, Whose sacred humanity is *the* window in the wall, says, "If you have seen me you have seen the Father" (Jn 14:9). A Priest should convey the same. By his life he should reveal to the faithful the Father they cannot see.

Further, *the window in the wall* is present without, in a sense, being present. It is there but serves its purpose best by calling attention not to itself but to what is beyond it. Now, both aspects pertain to the Priest. Like the window in the wall, he must be both there and not there.

He must be there after the example of our Lord in the Blessed Sacrament. We speak of the Real Presence of Christ in the Eucharist. We ought to speak also of the real presence of the Priest to his people. Saint John Vianney never tired of pointing towards the tabernacle and saying with great emotion, "He is there!" His words carried weight not only because they conveyed true doctrine but also because the *speaker* was really there. Because Saint John Vianney was present to them – in catechesis, in charitable works, most of all in the confessional – they could more easily believe that our Lord was there in the Eucharist.

Imitate what you celebrate. If a Priest desires his people to believe in the Real Presence of Jesus in the Eucharist, then he himself must be really present to them. By his own life and ministry he must approximate that presence of Christ. For the People of God to believe that "the Lord takes delight in his people" (Ps 149:4) and that "his delight is in the race of man" (Pr 8:31), they must have some hint of that delight from their Priests.

They must sense the desire of the Priest to be present, to be among them in all aspects of their lives – in their joys, sorrows, sufferings, and victories.

Because of his call to live among his people, the parish Priest in particular must approximate the Incarnation. He is to make known by his own presence the astounding truth that "the Word was made flesh and dwelt among us" (Jn 1:14). The temptation to escape – physically, mentally, or both – has always led to the absentee pastor. That is, the Priest who does the bare minimum, who functions merely as an administrator, or whose approach to the sacramental ministry is detached from any other contact with parishioners. By such behavior he disobeys the command he received to imitate what he celebrates.

In another sense, however, the Priest imitates the window in the wall by *not* being there. Centuries before Monsignor Knox, a greater theologian used another phrase that helps our reflections. In praise of the Sacred Host Saint Thomas Aquinas wrote, "Adoro te devote latens Deitas" – *Devoutly I adore Thee, O hidden God. Latens Deitas* – the hidden God. Our Lord's Eucharistic Presence, although substantial and real, remains nonetheless veiled under the form of bread. He is entirely present to us – not in His glory but in a humble, veiled, hidden mode. So also the Priest must be content to be veiled – to labor in a hidden, unseen manner for the salvation of souls.

Then-Cardinal Ratzinger once described his elaborate ordination and first Mass – how the celebrations went on for days and he was the focus of an entire town's festival. How he had to keep his wits about him, saying repeatedly, "This is not for you, Joseph, not for you." Saint Josemaria Escrivá had a different experience. His was a low-key ordination and simple first Mass (a Low Mass in a side chapel with a small congregation). In comparison to Father Ratzinger's celebration, Father Escrivá's may strike us as unfortunate, and in many ways it was. We should, after all, give our Lord great honor and adornment in the liturgy. We should celebrate a Priestly ordination fittingly. Yet the simplicity of Saint Josemaria Escrivá's ordination and first Mass has the virtue of reminding us that the Priest must be content in obscurity and hiddenness – like our Lord veiled in the form of bread.

At his ordination and for days – perhaps weeks – afterwards, a Priest receives tremendous attention and affection. The studies and formation are over. We ought to celebrate. He is now a Priest. But for every Priest there comes a day when no one congratulates him or asks for his blessing. When he has no dinner, no reception, no banquet to go to. When presents no longer arrive. When he finds himself in the regular, day-to-day work of a Priest – very much a hidden, obscure life, without grandeur or spotlights. When his words of counsel go unacknowledged. When his visit to the hospital goes unnoticed, perhaps even rejected. When his prayers for people go unknown. *Then* his ordination is more perfect – *then* he will be as our Eucharistic Lord, *latens Deitas*, as one hidden. Then he will be a better window in the wall – not calling attention to himself but giving people access to what is beyond.

A story about four Priests visiting Pope Saint Pius X conveys the dignity of Priestly obscurity. The Pope greeted each and asked what he did. The first introduced himself as a university professor. The second Priest served on the faculty of a seminary. The third practiced canon law in his chancery. The fourth Priest simply said, "Habeo curam animarum" – *I have the care of souls.* In a very beautiful way, he was telling the Pope that he was simply a parish Priest. When Pius X heard those words, he knelt before *that* Priest and asked for his blessing.

Every day we Priests take bread and wine and by the words of Consecration effect a miracle that even the angels cannot perform. May our lives be formed by that daily offering – that we not only sacrifice but be sacrificed, that we be the window in the wall bestowing divine light upon those in our care, that we be a hidden, veiled presence of the Father – that we be Priests after the Eucharistic Heart of Jesus.